Servant of God under four kings

DANIEL
Servant of God under four kings

Geoff Thomas

BRYNTIRION PRESS

Unless otherwise stated, Scripture quotations are from the Holy Bible, New International Version, 1984 edition. Used by permission of Hodder & Stoughton Ltd.

Cover design: Mike Fryer, Applications

Published by **Bryntirion** Press
Bryntirion, Bridgend CF31 4DX, Wales, UK
Printed by WBC Book Manufacturers, Bridgend

Contents

To

Esther Jones

Yr Odyn, Trefechan, Aberystwyth

my encouragement and exemplar

'A little one shall become a thousand,
and a small one a strong nation.'
(Isaiah 60:22)

Introduction

In 1998 the fiftieth Annual English Conference of the Evangelical Movement of Wales takes place. For much of this time the Conference has been held in the university town of Aberystwyth, at the heart of the Welsh Principality on its western coast. There, each August, two weeks of preaching take place, the first week in the English language and the second in Welsh. As the end of the century approaches about 1,300 people are in attendance during the English-language week. The meetings have had to move out of the largest chapel buildings in the town and up to the Great Hall on the University campus on Penglais Hill, under the shadow of which the small town nestles.

This is considered one of the principal preaching weeks in Europe, and that claim is demonstrated by the very structure of the Conference. There are prayer meetings attended by hundreds of people at the beginning of the morning, and then at 11 a.m. the single preaching meeting takes place in which the Conference Addresses are delivered. Complete freedom is given to the speaker in his choice of theme. He does not announce it until he stands before the congregation. He has ample time in four mornings to develop what he has to say, and is under no pressure other than the privilege and responsibility of the hour. He faces about seven hundred people under the age of twenty-five, and if they are edified the older people will be additionally helped in hearing the Word through those young ears. Many who have passed through the summer camps of the Evangelical Movement of Wales are armed with notebooks. No one could wish for a more sympathetic hearing. The preacher is especially settled by the great hymns of the faith being sung.

The five evening sessions again are a single meeting with one minister and one sermon, but the task of the different preachers is to declare with affection and conviction the gospel of the Lord Jesus Christ. The preaching is generally in the older Welsh way, that is, with such themes as the certainty of death, meeting with the living God, the need of the new birth, heaven and hell, all coming to the fore. It would be pleasant to report that the ministry during the weeks, in both the mornings and evenings, always met the expectations of the discerning crowds who gather. That is not the case. We are not living in days of extraordinary preaching, and that is what the age demands. But the failure is not through the weakness of expectation of those who plan or those who attend the Conference. 'The wind bloweth where it listeth,' said the Lord Christ to Nicodemus, 'and thou hearest the sound thereof, but canst not tell whence it cometh, and whither it goeth' (John 3:8 AV). There is a sovereignty in God's determination to bless his people, and we live in a Principality which is experiencing, with all the Western world, the strange work of God's judgment upon its sin. Whatever our weakness as preachers, this has not caused the organisers of the Conference to resort to the tricks of the world to make people happy. There is no appeal to the flesh, to the performances of men and women, to musical groups and drama slots. The Conference casts itself upon the Word and the Spirit. The organisers do not even resort to looking east across Offa's Dyke to orators

8

from England who will declaim, and pat us Welsh boys on the head for trying our best, and then speed back to England after the preaching is over, having shown us how to do it. No. The preaching has to come very largely from men of Wales addressing their fellow country-men. And so the evening messengers have been men with such names as Andrew Davies, Gareth Davies, Graham Harrison, Vernon Higham, Peter Jeffery, Dennis Jenkins, Omri Jenkins, Hywel Jones, Hugh Morgan, Dafydd Morris, Luther Rees, Neville Rees, Derek Swann, Derek Thomas, John Thomas, Gwynn Williams, and others.

The morning speakers have come from further afield, from North America as well as from the British Isles. Al Martin, Douglas Kelly and Don Carson have come from the USA; Douglas MacMillan, James Philip, Donald MacLeod, Eric Alexander and Sinclair Ferguson have travelled from Scotland; J. I. Packer, Andrew Anderson, Brian Edwards, Paul Tucker and Sidney Lawrence are some of those who have come from England, and Edward Donnelly sailed and drove to Aberystwyth from Ireland. There have also been help-ful conference addresses given by a number of the above Welsh preachers.

I was asked to join that company and to give the morning addresses in 1997. I felt that that was a great honour. I live in this town of Aberystwyth, having been a minister here for my single pastorate since the year 1965. During the weekend at the commencement of every Conference I preach to many people. It is a Sunday that our own small congregation anticipates, and afterwards talks about, enthusiastically.

How does one choose a subject for the Conference Addresses? I happened to be sitting in the Conference in 1996 listening to Sinclair Ferguson speak on the book of Ruth, and 'felt' I had to speak on Daniel the following year. The biblical rationale for this choice was that the themes of the book appeared to be so relevant for the Babylon in which we live, and for this youthful gathering. The reader can now judge that conviction. I had moments of uncertainty during the next year, thinking of alternatives, but always came back to that book. I had the opportunity to go through Daniel in our midweek meetings during the year, and then the month before the August Conference I shaped these four addresses. It was an awesome delight to give the following messages in that happy week.

What books are helpful for an understanding of the book of Daniel? The first is certainly the commentary of John Calvin. One man at present in membership in our Aberystwyth church is my friend Richard Davies. Converted at the age of twenty, within two years he was studying in a liberal theological seminary. It was a period of conflict on two levels. Firstly, on a spiritual level: there was no encouragement to any form of spiritual vitality, with little if any stimulation in discipleship. Secondly, on an intellectual level: 'How was I to reconcile what I believed with what I was being taught? It was here', he says, 'that I found J. Gresham Machen's *Christianity and Liberalism* to be an immense help. But on the spiritual level the Lord used the 800 pages of Calvin's *Commentary on the Book of Daniel* to revive my flagging soul.' Richard Davies learned six great lessons from this book:

1. The living God is superior to all idols and gods of this world. No one should feel ashamed of identifying with him.

2. God is in control. He is sovereign in history and prophecy.

3. God will be vindicated.

4. Christ's kingdom is a growing kingdom that will never be destroyed.

5. The importance of a holy life. God uses faithful consistent Christian living for his own glory.

6. Prayer is vital to the life of the true believer. The sixty-six extempore prayers of Calvin at the end of each 'lecture' are printed, and these were manna to my soul.

So John Calvin's commentary on Daniel, in print today by the Banner of Truth, is highly recommended. Richard Davies says, 'No book has encouraged me as this commentary. It has made Daniel my favourite book in the Bible.'

My teacher at Westminster Theological Seminary, Philadelphia, was Dr Edward J. Young, and his approach to the book of Daniel has become mine. His teaching is available in his commentary on Daniel published by the Banner of Truth. Another book which is a most helpful exposition of Daniel is Stuart Olyott's *Dare To Stand Alone* (Evangelical Press, 1982). With the experience of being a pastor in London and Liverpool as well as being a missionary in Lausanne—and in 1999 to become a lecturer in preaching at the Evangelical Theological College of Wales in Bryntirion—Stuart Olyott has the ability to make the more apocalyptic passages of Daniel lucid. There is not another commentary that makes the book so accessible.

My own favourite book on Daniel is my well-worn copy of *Dreams and Dictators* by the Dutch minister, the late Herman Veldkamp (Paideia Press, St Catherines,

Canada, 1978). Dr Theodore Plantinga has shown unerring judgment in the number of Dutch books he has translated into English. Herman Veldkamp served as a minister in the Reformed Churches in the Netherlands, and he has also written books on Amos, 1 & 2 Thessalonians and Jeremiah. Not commentaries, but showing a deep knowledge of the language and background of those books, Veldkamp's books are a series of systematic expository sermons preached to his own people. They are full of insight, and anyone who also reads *Dreams and Dictators* will see the source of many of my ideas. This good-hearted Welshman salutes his memory.

Finally, a word about the approach to the book of Daniel dictated by the structure of four mornings, and an hour on each occasion to exegete and draw out the lessons of twelve chapters of Scripture. Daniel served under four emperors in Babylon, from the time he was a teenage boy to great old age: Nebuchadnezzar, Belshazzar, Darius and Cyrus. I have divided the book into four sections, examining how Daniel lived his life under the pressures and opportunities to serve God which each of these four monarchs brought into his life.

1
Under Nebuchadnezzar
The battle for a young man

The first four chapters of Daniel describe four vivid incidents that took place during the reign of king Nebuchadnezzar. How this teenager, Daniel, came to be living so far from home, over 500 miles east of Jerusalem across the Syrian desert in Babylon, is explained to us in the opening verses of the book: 'In the third year of the reign of Jehoiakim king of Judah, Nebuchadnezzar king of Babylon came to Jerusalem and besieged it. And the Lord delivered Jehoiakim king of Judah into his hand' (Daniel 1:1-2). That unforgettable year for the people of God was 605 BC. Nebuchadnezzar had besieged Jerusalem and conquered it. God delivered his own rebellious and idol-loving people into exile and slavery. The Israelites had resisted all his entreaties spoken through many of his prophets, and so the Lord lifted his own rod of judgment— Nebuchadnezzar and his army—and smote Jerusalem. The vessels of the temple were taken to Babylon, to Nebuchadnezzar's gods and Nebuchadnezzar's temple. That is how conquerors acted. They took possession of sacred artefacts and of people too.

What is chronicled in the remainder of the book of Daniel is a 70-year-long campaign, a war between Jerusalem and Babylon, between the kingdom of heaven and the kingdom of darkness, between harmony and chaos. You find this same conflict in the last book of the Bible, the book of Revelation. These two are there locked in combat—Babylon and the Jerusalem that descends from heaven. And that struggle goes on even today, a struggle that never ends, between the kingdom of Christ and the kingdom of Satan, between the church and the world, between the Lord and antichrist. Christians are at war, and this Old Testament book telling of the life of Daniel is inspirational and exemplary in helping us in that strife.

1. Daniel draws a line (chapter 1)

When you read the first chapter, one fact leaps out at you: it was a struggle for young people. Daniel and his friends are in their early teens, and they have to bear the brunt of the onslaught. The attack is very cunning. There is here no siege with an entrenched army, embankments, battering rams and catapults. Babylon already has their bodies captive, and now wants their minds too. Nebuchadnezzar desires their young but eternal souls, their whole personalities, their wills, their affections. He wants them to dress as they dress in Babylon, to speak as they speak in Babylon, to behave as they behave in Babylon, and even to eat what they eat in Babylon. He wants them to feel and think and enthuse about what they feel and think and enthuse about in Babylon. Nebuchadnezzar wants conformity throughout his dominion. He wants to 'Babylonise' everyone, and his approach is very subtle and very determined. 'We'll get the children', Nebuchadnezzar says; 'we'll get them when they are young, and then in their whole lives they will serve us.'

So Nebuchadnezzar sends Ashpenaz the chief of his

court officials on a mission. He is to bring the cream of the young men of Israel, the smartest boys, all the future leaders of the Lord's people, to the royal palace. Imagine it! Not having to live any longer with the slave peoples in the ghettos of Babylon but in the royal palace itself! That is where you are going to find the future leaders of the people of God, and what can the church accomplish without leaders? Here are these vulnerable young men, away from their parents, impressionable boys, their convictions not settled—and not in a concentration camp, not in the Gulag, where a rod of steel would be put in their backbones and not only survival but revolution plotted in the dark nights! You find them in the palace—intelligent boys, given books and teachers, promised vocations and job satisfaction, careers and leadership, and an escape from this slave status—treated like aristocrats in the Eton of Babylon!

Nebuchadnezzar wanted them Babylonians in heart and spirit, body and soul. He wanted them alienated from the Lord and utterly marinated in Babylonian ideals, assimilating that culture's whole way of life and values, forgetting all their past. What they laughed about, and what they would lay down their lives for, would henceforth be Babylonian. To see the world just as Babylonians saw it was the king's aim, and his people-control touched the smallest areas of their lives, even their diets. How important is food? When we go to a foreign country we are struck by the language, the dress, the climate, the vegetation—and the food. 'They don't eat proper food', we think. What we eat is a form of self-expression. So we are told (v.5) that 'The king assigned them a daily amount of food and wine from the king's table.' It was not a luxurious diet, but the food was on a Babylonian menu, with Babylonian herbs

15

and spices flavouring it, prepared and set on the tables by Babylonian hands. It did not taste like Jerusalem food. Everything about these boys had to change. And the old-fashioned approach to eating and drinking that they had received from their parents had to go. All the threads tying them to the past had to be broken. That life back in Israel, and the values of God's people that they had brought to the Babylonian ghetto, were all to be annihilated one by one.

It was at this issue of the food that Daniel drew a line. When he was being trained in 'the language and literature of the Babylonians' (v.4), he didn't protest. And when they were given new names (v.7), he didn't protest. But when Daniel was put on a new diet (v.8), he would not conform. Christians are going to meet many things in state schools and universities with which they do not agree. But we are not a people who want a reputation for protesting at every single thing we disagree with, are we? Not every issue is a 'no surrender' issue, is it? We are not putting our hands up in classes to draw the teachers' eyes to our protests at everything we think might be against what our parents and church have taught us. Our teachers know far more than we know, and young people have to pray to God for wisdom to know the issues over which they are going to take a stand. Daniel didn't protest when they called him 'Belteshazzar', even though it was a name of a Babylonian idol. 'If they want to call me that, well, they can call me that. Sticks and stones may break my bones, but nicknames never hurt me', he could have said to his sore friends when they raised their eyebrows at these ugly foreign names. They will call *us* names too, won't they?—'God-squad', 'the squeaky-clean brigade', 'fundies', 'Holy Joe', 'the Wee Frees', 'the Preacher

Boy', 'the Bishop'. We keep smiling. A mother might say to a pastor, 'They call my son names in school and laugh at him because he is a Christian.' The pastor will tell her that it is a very sad life if a Christian is never laughed at. Jesus said, 'Blessed are you when people insult you' (Matthew 5:11). So Daniel kept sweet, and yet he carefully drew the line at the imposed food and resolved he would not indulge.

It is important to draw the line at the crucial issue, and then not to give way. A story is told of a Territorial Army group that went on manoeuvres every six months over a weekend. They stayed in barracks, and always one of the men would come back from the village pub half-drunk on the Saturday night. He would stagger into the dormitory towards midnight and would stand in the middle of the room. Then he would draw a line across the floor and shout to the men, 'I challenge any of you to cross this line.' He did this every six months for a few years, and the men would groan and turn over and try to get back to sleep. But one of the newer men had had enough of this. He got out of bed, walked up to the line and crossed it. The drunk looked at him; he was a big, mean-looking fellow. The drunk hesitated, and then he took the piece of chalk and drew another line further down. We have all seen Christian organisations, agencies and denominations who have said that they've drawn a line and they don't intend to cross it. The issue has been some so-called non-negotiable point of Christian teaching, or some Christian ethic. Then some big man, with charm or qualifications or a following, has come and has defiantly crossed that line; and they have capitulated and moved the line, with lame excuses.

Young Daniel wasn't in the business of moving the

line, and he drew the line at food. We might think that God isn't interested in food and water and soup and meat and vegetables. 'Come on now, Daniel, don't be awkward. Your attitude is a bit offensive. You know the Pharisees would also be fussy about food, ceremonially washing their hands before eating, and refusing to enter Pilate's court on a certain day in the week; and yet all the time the great sin was in their hearts of plotting murder against the Messiah.' But Daniel was not a Pharisee. He is filled with the Spirit of the Messiah. He saw the food as simply an outward sign of an anti-Jehovahist system, and that his whole way of life was being radically transformed and replaced. The menu wasn't accidental. People say to us today that they admire our religion and they are glad that it has worked for us, but that religion is a private matter. King Nebuchadnezzar would laugh if he heard that, because, for him, all of life was permeated by religion. Every meal in the royal palace was a holy meal. Everything was a gift of Nebuchadnezzar's gods. Like the victory over Israel and its God which his gods had secured, so they continued to provide for him length of life and daily food.

The meals were presided over by the priests of Babylon, and whenever you had a meal, thanks were given to the gods who provided this food. You might sprinkle some pepper or spices as a thanksgiving to the gods before you ate. Young Daniel recognised the challenge: 'What harmony is there between Christ and Belial? . . . What agreement is there between the temple of God and idols?' (2 Corinthians 6:15-16). So Daniel defined it. There was danger in that dining hall. Of course, there is danger in the lions' den, but there is danger too in restaurants. Being bought by expense account meals and clinking glasses, and someone else paying the bill, and your stomach becoming Satan's ally—is that not a danger? Daniel drew the line at the food. It was as if he saw the lions in the king's banqueting hall. If Daniel hadn't been faithful there, he would not have survived the lions' den. Few will. If you eat with Belial, then the lions are going to eat you. Young Christians sometimes think, How could I cope with martyrdom? How could I cope with wild beasts in the arena? Would I stand? The answer to such questions is, How are you managing today? How do you behave at the end-of-term dinner, or the office party at Christmas? How do you manage at school? on the football field? in the changing rooms? Why do you torment yourselves about lions' dens in distant places when you are failing in the dining room today?

Daniel 1 is a sad chapter. How many hundreds of young men came from Jerusalem to Babylon? How many had discernment? How many took their stand? Just four, a mere four. And if Daniel hadn't articulated the danger, would the other three have done so? Hasn't the church been blessed because a man has seen the issue? C. H. Spurgeon saw a down-grade amongst English Baptists in the 1880s. In 1893, two Highland ministers, Donald Macfarlane and Donald Macdonald, saw the theological decline in the Church of Scotland. Gresham Machen defined and fought error in Princeton Seminary in the opening decades of the century. In a local congregation things may be slipping, and one man has gathered the deacons around him and explained to them the issues. One man has seen the consequences of what is being said and done. There in Babylon is this crowd of teenagers; they are all professing Old Testament Messiahists—and they have all fallen

19

into line and tuck in to Babylonian food: 'You've got to give and take, haven't you?' they say. 'Why be awkward? Don't rock the boat, Daniel. Do you want to go back to the ghetto? We can accomplish so much more by a little flexibility.' So they all agree—except these four boys. They were convinced of the impossibility of what they were being asked to do: to partake of that meal, with its false sacramentalism and idolatry.

What did Daniel do? He certainly didn't have a martyr's complex. He wasn't pigheaded or surly. He simply asked permission not to eat, and he did this so graciously! Daniel went to see the proper man. He took his courage into his hands and, as a 14-year-old boy, he asked if they might be excused from partaking of the appointed food. The chief official's initial response was that if he granted Daniel's request it would cost him his life. 'If you look pale and emaciated and the king discovers you have not been eating this food . . . it will be curtains for me.' But Daniel wouldn't be put off. 'Just give us a trial for ten days', he said. 'See how we'll be in that time.' The man thought, 'Well, there's no harm in that. They are going to be here three years! I can give them ten days.' 'All right,' he says. It was just as easy as that! With Daniel and the others fearing the worst, this Babylonian turned out to be as pleasant as could be. The boys discovered they had the boss on their side. What sort of God was theirs? Even the heart of king Nebuchadnezzar was in their Lord's hands. It was a great discovery for young men to make in Babylon.

So, we are saying, be wise as to which issues you are going to draw a line about, and always ask the Lord for help; and then be as courteous and as gracious as you can be in approaching people. I would even encourage you not to write letters, but rather, if it is possible, to see someone and talk to them. There's a lot of power in a stammering tongue. Consider the result here: the chief official was won over, and at the end of ten days there was a glow of health on Daniel, Shadrach, Meshach and Abednego. God blesses those who obey, and he promises to spread a table before us in the presence of our enemies. Daniel chapter one is urging us to remember the very simple rules for Christian living. 'Love your neighbour as yourself.' Do it! More, 'Love God with all your heart.' Do it! 'Be as wise as a serpent and as harmless as a dove.' Do it! Don't admire these precepts. Do them! And the chapter ends with the words, 'And Daniel remained there until the first year of King Cyrus' (v.21).

Satan's plan was that Daniel wouldn't stay the course, that he wouldn't be God's great prophet speaking up in Babylon. Satan's plan was to assist Nebuchadnezzar, so that everything about the Lord disappeared: his name, his law, his covenant, the record of his mighty works, and his people—all gone. But God's plan was different, for it was that this young boy Daniel, who was taken as a slave and a refugee to Babylon, should have an extraordinary influence in that empire. The last verse of this chapter says he was there until the first year of king Cyrus. Do you understand that?—seventy-five years later and he's still there! Nebuchadnezzar is forgotten, but Daniel is there. Kings have been coming and going, world empires rising and falling, but Daniel is still there until the first year of king Cyrus. What an unforgettable year that first year of Cyrus was, when an edict was passed that God's people could return to Jerusalem, and the people could take down their harps from the willows and sing because they were going home! The greatest single reason why, in seventy years' time, God's people still existed as an entity in Babylon was because Daniel had refused to eat the king's food. Through the grace of God this boy knew some things better than the greatest men in all the world.

2. The fears of Babylon (chapter 2)

If chapter 1 reveals the powerful single-mindedness of Babylon, the second chapter displays its impotence. Certainly it was no rebellion, no internal strife, no new enemy marching on Babylon with a vast army, that characterised those days. Nebuchadnezzar was as much in control as ever. Nothing had changed outwardly. If a visitor came, he would see a triumphant, prosperous nation at peace. What he did not know was that Nebuchadnezzar was in a torment because of the recurrence of a dream. Now we all dream, and our dreams are generally unmemorable fancies. In his hymn 'Our God, our help in ages past', Isaac Watts writes:

> Time, like an ever-rolling stream,
> Bears all its sons away;
> They fly forgotten, as a dream
> Dies at the opening day.

Dreams are evanescent and unreal. But one dream that refused to die at dawn caused uproar in Babylon. It almost wiped out the intellectuals. It certainly shook up everything and everyone. Does our God's sovereignty stretch to dreams? The king was deeply upset. His mind was obsessed by a constant nightmare, and he soon dreaded the night hours. So he took out his frustration on his wise men: 'Now, you smart fellows, tell me what dream I've had, and then also give me its interpretation', he said savagely. They looked at him in astonishment: 'No king, however great and mighty, has ever asked such a thing of any magician or enchanter or astrologer' (v.10). What if your neighbour turned to you and held a pistol against your head, saying, 'Tell me the dream I had last night!'? They were terrified, because the king proceeded to order their summary execution (vv.12-13).

This is what God can do with a dream. It is lighter than a cobweb, and just as flimsy; yet death threatened Daniel and all the cream of the intelligentsia of the empire because of a dream. If a dream from God can do that, what will it be when God himself comes? How easy it is to terrify strong men outside of Christ! Why do all the famous people have to go out with body-guards? Why did Tiger Woods request armed guards when he took part in his first British Open? Why do film stars live in fortresses? Why do Presidents drive about in bulletproof limousines? Because they are all terrified of what might just happen to them. This absolute monarch, the mightiest man in the whole world, was scared because he saw his future. Daniel tells him, 'Your mind turned to things to come . . . what is going to happen' (v.29). Nebuchadnezzar, through his network of spies, knew everything that was going on in palace, city and empire, but he didn't want to face up to the unavoidable future. Yet the dream insisted that he dwell on that, and his cruelly bought peace vanished.

Nebuchadnezzar's dream was a revelation from God. The voice of the Lord was saying to him that his throne was not an impregnable rock of ages. God started to rock this king, just a little, but night after night, and for Nebuchadnezzar it was like being on a ship in a storm. So what did he do? What do men of the world do when death comes and knocks on their door, and they start to look at their futures? As they shower they find a lump, and they think of their futures; or they get a new chest pain as they climb the old hill, and they think of their futures; or God takes someone from them, and they think of their futures. What lies before them?

What do men do at such times? Unless grace intervenes, they begin to look to other men; they do not look towards the living God. They look to the wits of men to deal with the unknown future. Nebuchadnezzar's dream drove him to man. He cried, 'Send for my men, the magicians, enchanters, sorcerers and astrologers, to tell me what I've dreamed.' That's what the world does. What's going to happen in the new millennium? Send for the futurologists and the stargazers. Let the experts give us a printout as to what may happen. But Nebuchadnezzar's wise men were speechless at this request. They said, 'First, tell us the dream; give the text and we'll exegete it.' Nebuchadnezzar was no fool. Anyone can give a prophecy. It doesn't take much imagination to cobble together sweet-sounding promises about the future. But here were his experts who claimed to be in touch with the heavens, men who knew the meaning of life. They said they could predict the future. They were intimate with his victory-giving gods—weren't they? Surely it was not difficult for men who knew the gods to be smart enough to tell him the dream itself, as well as the interpretation. This was a test of their authority, set by the king. Nebuchadnezzar would not play ball; he wanted to be told the dream first, as a proof that their interpretation would be true truth. He grimly shook his head and sent out his execution squad to round up all the smart men of the kingdom (v.13). The whole academic community was at its wits' end; the government was in crisis, and all the might and wisdom of Babylon were shown to be bankrupt.

Many men will give us their ideas about the future. Some will speak about death and what lies beyond it. There are even men within the professing church who, for their own fancies, will dismiss the resurrection of the dead. What authority do they have for their theories to be believed? At the University of Chicago Divinity School there has been an annual 'Baptist Day' for many years, when leaders of that denomination in Illinois are invited to the School. Their support is encouraged, and those who go bring their packed lunches and sit and eat together on a grassy knoll in between listening to theologians. One year the Divinity School invited the late Dr Paul Tillich to speak. Tillich was born in Germany in 1886, and in 1933 he went to Union Seminary, New York. On that 'Baptist Day', Tillich lectured on the resurrection of Christ, giving his restitution theory: that the resurrection took place in the 'ecstatic' experience of the disciples, and that it restored Jesus to the dignity of the Christ in their own minds; that it probably belonged to the time prior to Peter's confession, but it was not an event belonging to the time after the death of Jesus. Tillich told them that the resurrection of the body was a symbol expressing the truth of 'essentialisation', and that heaven and hell were to be taken seriously, but not literally. The lecture was long, almost two hours, and given with a strong German accent. Then there was a question time. An old minister rose to his feet: 'Docta Tilick, I got a question.' The congregation turned around and looked at him. He slowly lifted an apple out of his lunch bag and took a bite. There was an embarrassing pause. 'Docta Tilick . . . my question is very simple *(munch, munch)* . . . I don't know much about essentialisation, nor about this restitution theory *(crunch, crunch)* . . . and I don't speak a word of German . . . All I wanna know is this . . . This apple I'm eating *(chew, chew)* . . . is it bitter or is it sweet?' The plain white-haired man was old, and from a minority race, and so he could not be belittled. In exemplary scholarly fashion Dr Tillich replied courteously, 'I cannot possibly answer that question, for I haven't tasted your apple.' The white-haired preacher dropped the remains of the apple into his lunch bag, looked at Dr Paul Tillich and said calmly, 'Neither have you tasted my Jesus.' There was a smattering of applause in the room.

What authority does any man have to speak of death and the future? Let's see something divine, that we may have grounds to believe them when they speak of our futures. The Lord Jesus Christ was speaking to a dense crowd of the possibility of the forgiveness of sins through entrusting themselves exclusively into his safe keeping, when a paralysed man was lowered from the roof to his feet (Mark 2:1-12). 'Son, your sins are forgiven', said Jesus to him. 'Who can forgive sins but God only?' thought the experts looking on, hearing and judging everything. 'Which is easier,' said Jesus to them, 'to say, your sins are forgiven, or to say, take up your bed and walk?' We all know the answer to that question. To talk about forgiveness, and to give interpretations of dreams, and to say that resurrection and heaven and hell are symbols—all that is far easier to talk about than to speak to a paralysed man the words, 'Take up your bed and walk.' If a man says that, then all eyes are focused on the patient. Will he be healed? As they looked, the paralysed man got up, and the people were shown another proof of the divine authority of the Son of God through whom do come forgiveness of sins and eternal life.

Nebuchadnezzar was saying, 'Talk is cheap. Show me you are really in touch with the gods and can be trusted in predicting the future by telling me what my dream actually was.' But they were bankrupt. God gave a man a dream—just one constant dream—and it started to take apart what the mightiest military machine in the world had put together at such cost. There was no one amongst all the diviners who had that authority that comes from a true knowledge of the divine, to tell the king what his dream was. Many claimed they had that knowledge, but no one could prove it when it came to the test.

Now Nebuchadnezzar had an additional worry: not only the dream, but also the total failure of human wisdom. He was surrounded, he realised, by ambitious pretenders, and his solution to that dilemma was to wipe out the bourgeoisie. That's a familiar response: 'You've got a degree. You've got some office. You've got some influence. We're going to cut your heads off. Because it's you who are the dangerous, subversive people.' Haven't we heard it in our own century in Russia, in Cambodia, in China? There's the knock at the door in the night, and the secret police are taking people off in their cars, and your husband becomes one of the disappeared ones. It happens when the supremos fear for the future, have been let down, and distrust all their underlings.

A knock came on Daniel's door (v.13) when Daniel and his friends hadn't even been asked about the dream. The first time they found out about this brutality was when somebody was pulling them out saying,

27

'Come along. We knew where you lived.' But Daniel had learned from his first clash with Babylon what to do, and in the palace he appealed to the commander of the guard, asking Arioch if he were condemned to death, and why. 'Why did the king issue such a harsh decree?' (v.15). When he got the answer he went from the commander's presence to the king himself, for he had a special place in the king's affections. Nebuchadnezzar had found Daniel 'ten times better than all the magicians and enchanters in his whole kingdom' (1:20). Daniel asked the king, 'Give me some time. I'll tell you the dream, and I'll interpret it, but give me time.'

Daniel used the time so well. He didn't plot his escape. He didn't hold a conference with all the wise men. He said, 'Shadrach, Meshach, Abednego, come, we need to pray.' We must 'plead for mercy from the God of heaven concerning this mystery' (v.18). Four young men, four Old Testament Christians a long way from home, went down on their knees and spread out their predicament before God.

For years, young people in this town met on Friday afternoon at 4 o'clock. They weren't allowed to attend until they were 11 years of age, and the younger ones looked forward to the day when they would be able to join their older friends at the meeting. They came home from school and they prayed for an hour. They had been to the summer camps and had been blessed with the fellowship of young people in prayer, so they decided they would go on meeting together to pray. Over a period of ten years they gathered for an hour in different houses and prayed for God's name to be glorified and for God to bless their friends and churches. They were just a group of young people who made that

28

decision themselves. They didn't see a great awakening in Aberystwyth, but they saw their friends becoming Christians, and virtually all of them went on to be married in the Lord, and a lot of them continue to come to the Aberystwyth conferences each year with their spouses and children. Young people who meet and pray generally become contented adults who still meet and pray.

Daniel and his friends didn't ask for the interpretation of Nebuchadnezzar's dream. They desired the actual content of the dream, praying along the line of 'Lord, reveal to us the mystery. What dream did you give to Nebuchadnezzar? Grant us the knowledge of that revelation' (v.18). Nebuchadnezzar had gone to the wisdom of the world for help, but Daniel went to that Wisdom from above; he addressed the throne of the universe. Nebuchadnezzar wanted to destroy the people, but Daniel wanted to preserve them. That night the vision came; the revelation was given as Daniel slept (v.19). Nebuchadnezzar couldn't sleep, but Daniel could sleep as sweetly as Peter could sleep in prison— both of them with the threat of death hanging over them. Daniel could rest, and rise to praise God for his omnipotence, singing

Praise be to the name of God for ever and ever;
  wisdom and power are his.
He changes times and seasons;
  he sets up kings and deposes them.
He gives wisdom to the wise
  and knowledge to the discerning.
He reveals deep and hidden things;
  he knows what lies in darkness,
  and light dwells with him.

I thank and praise you, O God of my fathers:
  You have given me wisdom and power,
you have made known to me what we asked of you,
  you have made known to us the dream of the king.
(vv.20-23).

Then Daniel went to the commander of the guard and said, 'Don't start killing anyone. Take me to the king, and I will give the dream.' Nebuchadnezzar said with astonishment, or perhaps in scorn, 'Are you able to tell me what I saw in my dream and interpret it?' (v.26). 'No,' Daniel said. 'No man, not the wisest man on earth, can do that. What the future holds in store no one knows. I have no greater wisdom than other men.' But, he said, 'there is a God in heaven who reveals mysteries' (v.28). Daniel had been given the dream and its interpretation 'that you, O king, may know the interpretation' (v.30). God had not given his word in order for Daniel to meet with his circle of young friends and 'share' it with them, any more than God has given it to us for 'sharing sessions', but rather that we preach it before kings and nations. The Lord has given us a Book of wisdom about the future. What lies before us? What is death? What lies after death? What is the eternal state? How can I be safe? God has told us the answers to these questions. The Lord has shown himself in Christ, in his royal conquest of death and in his resurrection. What is ultimate reality? Is it death? Or is it Jesus Christ and that resurrection on the third day? The New Testament answer shows us that ultimate reality is not a coffin, and not a decaying corpse, but it is in him who is the resurrection and the life. That is the revelation we take to the whole world.

What was Nebuchadnezzar's dream? It was of a

huge statue standing like Blackpool tower, or even the CN Tower in Toronto, visible for miles around. Its head glistened in the sunshine because it was of gold; its chest and arms were of silver, its belly and thighs of bronze, its legs of iron, its feet partly iron and partly baked clay (vv.31-33). What kingdoms did that statue represent? The truth is that there is no kingdom it does not represent. It stands for every world dominion that man builds, every human empire and system, every power structure of man, all the great hegemonies of the ages. Sometimes they are gold, sometimes they are silver, sometimes they are bronze, sometimes they are clay—yet they are always the same. Men make them; men erect them; men prop them up—the shining gold of the Renaissance and the Enlightenment, the silver of the Celtic civilisations, the steel of the Iron Curtain, the clay of the Berlin Wall. They were different in Daniel's day. They will be different in the future. But they are not like a mountain; they are like the heroic statues that men have erected all over the world to celebrate their own prowess.

Nebuchadnezzar is given the application of the dream to his own age: 'You are that head of gold' (v.38), and after him other kingdoms, probably Babylon, Medo-Persia, Greece and Rome. But the king, together with them all, will be shattered into smithereens by a rock 'cut out, but not by human hands' (vv.34, 45). That rock represents the Messiah; and its expansion as it 'became a huge mountain and filled the whole earth' (v.35) is the growth of the Messianic kingdom. It 'will never be destroyed . . . it will itself endure for ever' (v.44). The stone which the builders reject and have refused to build upon, thinking how fragile it looks, that very stone comes rumbling remorselessly and irresistibly on and

31

on, destroying man's great structures one by one, growing like a mighty mountain and triumphing over them. God made all mankind witness this as the twentieth century was closing: imposing structures, and the very statues of Eastern Europe, fell while the kingdom of God quietly expanded. It is still increasing; the stone from above must become a mountain.

Kings have boasted that they will build something which will last a thousand years, and they have been destroyed in less than a decade. The kingdom of our God and of his Son Jesus Christ is overwhelming. We gather here, thousands of miles away from Babylon, on the shores of the Irish Sea. Here we are, centuries after Daniel lived or even after they crucified the Lord Jesus Christ. They said as they put his body in a grave, 'Well, he won't bother us any longer.' Yet for us the greatest reality in all the world is that Son of God. He dwarfs us all, and we live for him. He has supplied to us the meaning of life. He is our forgiveness and our acceptance with God.

Men and women, what lies before every one of you is an open-ended encounter with the Rock of Ages. That is the next great stage of your eternal journey. We are on our way to that. There is an appointment that you are going to keep, and it is with this Rock. It destroys everything that resists it. Everything has to make room for this Omnipotence; it is going to fill the whole earth. And in that earth which he will fill, he will not be an intolerable execration, nor some filthy swear word. His name will be like perfume poured forth, the fragrance of the cosmos. One day there will be a multitude of ten thousand times ten thousand singing praise to the Rock of Ages that was cleft for them. Have you thought of that? Or are you like

children building sandcastles with your backs towards
the advancing tide?

3. The fiery trial (chapter 3)

The second chapter ends with Daniel's elevation as
'ruler over the entire province of Babylon . . . in charge
of all its wise men' (v.48). Yet we are told that he
'remained at the royal court' (v.49). Perhaps his work
took him away occasionally; but, whatever the reason,
he is totally absent from the famous incident recorded
in chapter 3. It is the only chapter in the book of Daniel
where he receives no mention. All the threat and fear
encountered in the second chapter have gone, and in
the first verse of the next chapter we are plunged into a
new conflict: 'King Nebuchadnezzar made an image of
gold, ninety feet high and nine feet wide, and set it up
on the plain of Dura in the province of Babylon.' It is an
uncompromising beginning to an uncompromising chapter. The worried faces in the nation have gone; Nebuchadnezzar has set that dream behind him: 'We are not
to think about nightmares, and empires collapsing, and
prophecies about the future. Kings shouldn't worry
about such things. Let's celebrate the great "now"!'
Nebuchadnezzar's generals may have just returned
with news of victories and imperial expansion. The
dream of the statue set up by man and shattered in
pieces is thrust to the back of the Babylonian collective
consciousness, except that it had sowed a seed in
Nebuchadnezzar's mind. The king did with it what
'ignorant and unstable people' always do with living
themes from the Bible—'distort [them] . . . to their own
destruction' (2 Peter 3:16). So Nebuchadnezzar would
have a statue made. Even more beautiful than the one

in his dream, this one would not have a mere head of gold, but it would be entirely of gold to the tips of its toes. The king had once said, 'Surely your God is the God of gods and Lord of kings' (2:47). But, I mean, who in the world wants to hold on to every vow they've given, and every promise they've made, and every such statement as 'I'll go to church every Sunday from now on'? How many people, in the manipulative atmosphere of modern worship services, have sung all those songs about the King and the kingdom, with words just like those Nebuchadnezzar used—'He is King of kings and Lord of lords'—and yet very soon afterwards have set up some idol for themselves? Nebuchadnezzar was not the first great man in the world to change his mind about God, nor the last.

So Nebuchadnezzar has this statue erected. He will worship a power greater than Daniel's God, and he will make others worship it too. He'll make the whole empire worship it. This statue stands for the power of Babylon that Nebuchadnezzar has acquired and embodies. 'I am Babylon', he thinks. And when men see the sun shining on this, they will fall before this idol. It is built on the plain of Dura, i.e. 'the fortress'. 'A mighty fortress is the power of Babylon'—that is the statue's message. It is, in Hebrew measurements, 60 cubits high and 6 cubits wide. In the book of Revelation the number 'six' is important. The antichrist also had a great statue, and the beast's number is 666. So here in the plain of 'the fortress' is something demonic, harsh and blinding. And the people have to leave their families and their work and plod to Dura, gathering from all the empire—'men of every language' (v.4)—to boost the golden king's ego and bow before his statue, giving honour to it as to a god.

The worship of this idol is described; it is orchestrated and controlled to the last detail. 'This is what you are commanded to do, O peoples, nations and men of every language: As soon as you hear the sound of the horn, flute, zither, lyre, harp, pipes and all kinds of music, you must fall down and worship the image of gold that King Nebuchadnezzar has set up. Whoever does not fall down and worship will immediately be thrown into a blazing furnace' (vv.4-6). Who is there? Simply everybody: 'the satraps, prefects, governors, advisers, treasurers, judges, magistrates, and all the other provincial officials' (v.2)—everybody who was anybody. 'We'd better be there, even with our broken ankles, our old age, our influenza. We are not going to be noticed as absentees. We'll be there by hook or by crook.' What happened when they gathered on the plain? They 'dedicated' the idol (v.3): that is, they gave it personality. Orators spoke about it—what it had done already and what it could do. They bragged about it and sought to make it live. They spoke about it as if it were a living entity with some actual powers of its own—as if it could answer prayer, protect you, give you prosperity, bring your husband back safely from war, cure your diseases and give you children. This gold statue was to become the focus of the religion of the state: 'We are worshipping the great power of Babylon that has made us mighty. They don't push us around in the world any longer, thanks to this great golden figure.'

A group came to the front to commence the proceedings and create a religious atmosphere, carrying a whole range of musical instruments. And how they played! One wonders how they managed in the New Testament church, without a single musical instrument

35

mentioned in the Gospels or the book of Acts or the Epistles! That was a church like the unhewn rock, growing in vitality and energy and filling the whole world (Colossians 1:6). Yet there is no mention of an instrument, and when in the book of Acts a reference is made to Christians singing, it is to two men in prison at midnight (Acts 16:25), and that is virtually it (cf. Ephesians 5:19). But on the plain of Dura the band walks in and starts to play, and immediately people fall down. And if they didn't, they knew what would happen; they would be thrown into a blazing furnace. It was safe to be there and to fall down when the music played. The leader had conditioned them to that response with a dark threat thrown in (v.6).

The warning of a 'blazing furnace' is the give-away. We all know in this hideous century about death ovens, napalm bombs and incendiaries, torture chambers and *Schindler's List*. Nebuchadnezzar's threat of the fiery furnace for any foolish non-conformist is the indicator that blows the cover on the whole Babylonian system. It was just another tyranny, a despot's merciless machine. No one was gathering on the plain of Dura voluntarily. Not one person fell down before the statue because they had an atom of love in their hearts for the idol. Nebuchadnezzar had a beautiful city, with hanging gardens and an orchestra, and now another icon, an impressive golden statue; but the king had to force people to fall and worship, with the threat of the furnace if they declined. Nebuchadnezzar was a monster. The roaring furnace belching out its smoke was a symbol of this despot, while all through the vast crowd were scattered his secret police—the so-called 'astrologers' (v.8)—checking out on who might be sort-of crouching but not actually falling down flat.

Also in the crowd are Shadrach, Meshach and Abednego, administrators over the province of Babylon. They know why they have been summoned to Dura. They have heard the instructions and know the threat. They listen to the music, and they see everyone else getting down and lying before the statue. But they remain erect, with just a little glance at one another. They stand out as plain as three pikestaffs on the plain of Dura. These three Old Testament Messiahists know the law of God, and how it begins: 'Thou shalt have no other gods before me. Thou shalt not make unto thee any graven image, or any likeness of any thing that is in heaven above, or that is in the earth beneath, or that is in the water under the earth: thou shalt not bow down thyself to them, nor serve them' (Exodus 20:3-5 AV). The words are utterly lucid. The law of God is amongst the most easily understandable parts of Scripture. There was no problem of inadequate guidance. They knew what God required of them, and as everyone bowed to the ground like corn blown in the wind, these three young men remained erect.

The secret police ran straight to Nebuchadnezzar, basking in the glow of the occasion. 'O king, live for ever! You have issued a decree, O king . . . But there are some Jews whom you have set over the affairs of Babylon—Shadrach, Meshach and Abednego—who pay no attention to you, O king. They neither serve your gods nor worship the image of gold you have set up' (vv.9-12). Nebuchadnezzar was furious with rage. Here are two kingdoms—two empires—in total contradiction to one another. The kingdom of Nebuchadnezzar has no place for those who will not sing the songs of the pagan choir and kneel before this idol.

When the young men were brought to him he

recognised them and called them by name. These were the boys who had ten times the wisdom, dependability and integrity of all those toadies who sniffed around him for promotion. So he quizzed them: 'Is this true? Are you ready to worship the great golden god now? If so, very good. We will just forget about this momentary lapse. If not, there's the blazing furnace—I've made that plain. And what god is really able to rescue you from my hand?' (v.15). The men had learnt graciousness and they replied so gently: 'O Nebuchadnezzar, we do not need to defend ourselves before you in this matter. If we are thrown into the blazing furnace, the God we serve is able to save us from it, and he will rescue us from your hand, O king. But even if he does not, we want you to know, O king, that we will not serve your gods or worship the image of gold you have set up' (vv.16-18). They had not given in to the temptation to justify falling before the idol through reasoning with one another, 'Well, it's no big deal to bow down. It's just a cultural matter, just a courtesy, a declaration that we are giving to Nebuchadnezzar the things that are Nebuchadnezzar's.' Every other Jew there on the plain of Dura had argued himself into prostration, but these three were different. They had been taught by God that to him who knows what the good is and refuses to do it, to him that is sin (James 4:17). So the furnace was heated up seven times hotter than usual, and they were thrown into its glowing intensity by the strongest soldiers, who were killed in the process by arms of flame that leapt out at them.

There are two things of significance here. *The first is what happened in the flames*. The boys were tied up and thrown, in their clothes, into the furnace. But the house that the Lord is establishing in the world is not made of kindling wood and oil. God's people are not like a truckload of pigs taken to the slaughterhouse for their throats to be cut. You can't destroy the church in as matter-of-fact a way as men put down an old dog. There are thunders in heaven when the apple of the Lord's eye is touched on earth. When Nebuchadnezzar goes along to see the fun, hear the screams and watch the writhing agonies, his eyes pop out; for he surveys four men in the furnace, not three, all unbound and unharmed. That is the first reality confronting him within a stone's throw of that tall, dead idol. The Almighty who disturbs by sending dreams can himself come close in visiting his people, and he 'looks like a son of the gods' (v.25). It was enough to make Nebuchadnezzar jump with shock (v.24). The uninvited God whom he was seeing had more power than anything taking place that day on the plain of Dura. Those three who refused to bow to his idol were being visited by one of the race of the gods. He had not descended on the statue, nor shown himself to its worshippers, but he visited those three and turned that furnace into a pleasant morning stroll.

That was all Nebuchadnezzar was able to see with the physical eye, but what do we see when we flood this passage with the light of Calvary? Don't we see the Son of God in the furnace? Do our minds turn to Golgotha? Do we think of how the Lord Jesus Christ, in visiting us, entered the lake of fire there for us? The flames of hell can never go out, but the Lord Christ voluntarily enters into Calvary's hell for us, that we might walk the cool glades of heaven in peace with him, upon the green pastures and by its still waters for ever and ever. There is the Son of God in the furnace in Babylon, and he is there to protect every hair on the heads of his people—with whom he stands in the closest solidarity: 'Nebuchadnezzar, Nebuchadnezzar, why persecutest thou me?' Babylon decides it will hold a festival on the plain of Dura to celebrate its power: God determines to hold a festival on the hill of Golgotha to commemorate his grace. While the whole world falls down and is worshipping man, the church, in the smallest remnant of three boys, stands amazed in the presence of Jesus the Nazarene. The one who, on the cross, entered into the everlasting fires is present where three gather together in his name. Immediately there are four. What a difference a pervasive consciousness of this blessing would bring to all our gatherings! When a Christian husband and wife come together, then a third is there to bless and help them. Fourteen ministers met for a Prayer Retreat for pastors. One had been touched by these words of the New York pastor, Gardiner Spring:

The time was, when the pastors of the American churches valued the privilege of prayer. They were not only men of prayer, but they prayed often for and with one another. Their reciprocal and fraternal visits were consecrated and sweetened by prayer, nor was it anything unusual for them to employ days of fasting and prayer together for the effusions of God's Spirit upon themselves and their churches. They were days of power; days when God's arm was made bare, and his right hand plucked out of his bosom. Nor was it difficult to see, then, wherein lay the great strength of the pulpit. 'He that is feeble among them . . . shall be as David; and the house of David shall be as God' (Zechariah 12:8).

The prayer retreat those words inspired exceeded the

expectations of all who attended because of a fifteenth Person powerfully present with them.

The second point is simply this: that *Shadrach, Meshach and Abednego did not know in advance whether God would deliver them.* If saving them would advance his glory, then he would. 'God is able to save us' (v.17)—that is what they said. But since they had first turned from their sins and cast themselves on the mercy of God, they had known that the Holy One of Israel was also a God who in his majestic rectitude consumed those who loved sin. They had forfeited everything by their sin and the sin of their father Adam, and all they had received in their lives was by the grace of a merciful God. 'God is able to save us—but we have no claim on him that he will save us.' If he does not deliver us we will still obey the Lord: 'we want you to know, O king, that we will not serve your gods or worship the image of gold you have set up' (v.17).

That is the test, isn't it? And that is just where we are now. You have been told of men who have refused to work on Sundays and they get promotion. You go to Christian Businessmen's lunches and hear a man saying how he tithes all his profits and the Lord has doubled his turnover. You hear women testifying that they would not consider marrying those who had no interest in the Lord Jesus Christ and that God provided them with fine Christian husbands. Such things happen again and again. We have heard the preachers say, 'You give the Lord £10, and he will give £100 to you.' It is good psychology, but it is bad theology. We serve the Lord for nothing at all. Indeed, every Christian has to face up to the alternative possibility, that 'even if he does not deliver us' we will still do his will—serving Christ for loss, serving Christ for loneliness, serving Christ for

41

death. We don't have to be rich; we don't have to marry; we don't have to become parents; we don't have to live; but *we have to obey*. There is no way that we can worship a golden idol, come what may. What we are promised is that all grace will always abound, that God will supply all our need, and that the Son of God will never leave us. Yea, though we walk through the valley of the shadow of death, we will fear no evil, for he will be with us. If we are placed in the crucible, he will be there too. We have to remember that God often puts his people upon the altar and sustains them there. There is always a furnace for the church. There was a furnace in Egypt, in Babylon, in Rome, in the sixteenth century, in the eighteenth century, and there has been a furnace in the twentieth century. Whatever God has for his church in the next millennium, we can be guaranteed that there is going to be a furnace there too. Even when the signs of the appearing of Christ are at hand, because the antichrist, the 'man of sin', has appeared, there will be another furnace for the church.

Today God is calling us to be prepared. When you must draw a line, then don't rub it out and draw another line. I ask you, Where was true joy and lasting pleasure to be found on that day in Babylon? Was it found amongst those whose noses were in the dirt lying before a statue? Or was it found in those walking with the Son of God in the furnace? Every Christian knows the answer. The life lived under the cross of Christ is a life of joy. Don't let appearances fool you.

> Since all that I meet
>   Shall work for my good,
>   The bitter is sweet,
>   The medicine is food;

Though painful at present,
'Twill cease before long,
And then, O how pleasant
The conqueror's song!
(John Newton, 1705–1807)

Daniel chapter 3 ends with the strangest benediction you ever heard—from king Nebuchadnezzar! When I read this benediction, 'Praise be to the God of Shadrach, Meshach and Abednego, who has sent his angel and rescued his servants!' (v.28), then I feel as I do when I'm watching a state occasion on television and seeing the government or members of the royal family. The cameras are trained on them and they are singing great words like

The King of love my Shepherd is,
Whose goodness faileth never;
I nothing lack if I am His,
And He is mine for ever.

—and I am saying in my heart, 'O that in the muddle of your private lives it might be so for you!'

What Nebuchadnezzar is doing at the end of chapter 3 is to change the status of God-fearing men and women throughout the whole of his empire. 'I decree that the people of any nation or language who say anything against the God of Shadrach, Meshach and Abednego be cut into pieces and their houses be turned into piles of rubbish' (v.29). God used three young men, Shadrach, Meshach and Abednego, to preserve his church in Babylon. So this affirmation 'Their God is the greatest' becomes, at least temporarily, the agenda for the minds of the empire. It was on that day—the day when the

43

statue of gold was set up in the plain of Dura and everyone who was anyone was summoned there to worship it—that this very proclamation was made, that no god other than the God of Shadrach, Meshach and Abednego 'can save in this way' (v.29).

But, with all these fine sentiments, Nebuchadnezzar never destroyed the golden idol. It still stood there, a dead hearer of those living words (but only words) from the king. The Lord once said, 'These people . . . honour me with their lips, but their hearts are far from me' (Isaiah 29:13). 'The King of love my Shepherd is'—just words? 'No other God can save in this way'—just words? Or the deepest reality of all? Where are our hearts? Given to him?

And what was to happen to Nebuchadnezzar?

4. An imperial proclamation (chapter 4)

God's long-suffering towards king Nebuchadnezzar was further extended in three more striking mercies recorded for us in the fourth chapter of Daniel. The first came in the form of *a special revelation from God* by means of another dream that terrified the king (v.5). The vivid image that came to his unconscious mind was of a tree of singular size and beauty: 'before me stood a tree in the middle of the land. Its height was enormous. The tree grew large and strong and its top touched the sky; it was visible to the ends of the earth. Its leaves were beautiful, its fruit abundant, and on it was food for all. Under it the beasts of the field found shelter, and the birds of the air lived in its branches; from it every creature was fed' (vv.10-12). In the barren, desert-like landscape of much of Babylon such a tree was a magnificent sight. It was the grandest tree the world had ever seen, and as Nebuchadnezzar floats along in his dreams and contemplates it, did he modestly think, 'Just like me, yes, just like me!'?

The dream, though, soon turned into a nightmare, as Nebuchadnezzar saw a messenger descending from heaven and giving the order for the tree to be chopped down. 'Cut down the tree and trim off its branches; strip off its leaves and scatter its fruit. Let the animals flee from under it and the birds from its branches. But let the stump and its roots, bound with iron and bronze, remain in the ground, in the grass of the field' (vv.14-15a). The tree is not uprooted; it is allowed to live, but all that is beautiful and useful about it is gone. Still alive, what remains is a mere stump, little taller than the grass that surrounds it. Surely the great Nebuchadnezzar is not to be cut down? Yet 'all flesh is as grass, and all the glory of man as the flower of grass. The grass withereth, and the flower thereof falleth away: but the word of the Lord endureth for ever' (1 Peter 1:24-25 AV). The interpretation given by the 'messenger' in the vision applied directly to the king. He was soon to be brought as low as a man has ever been brought: 'Let him be drenched with the dew of heaven, and let him live with the animals among the plants of the earth. Let his mind be changed from that of a man and let him be given the mind of an animal, till seven times pass by for him' (vv.15b-16). The courts of heaven had decreed it would be so, not as a whim of their sovereignty, but so that the world might learn one lesson from the great king's fall: 'so that the living may know that the Most High is sovereign over the kingdoms of men and gives them to anyone he wishes and sets over them the lowliest of men' (v.17).

Nebuchadnezzar went immediately to the wisest men

in the kingdom, but all furtively pleaded ignorance as to its meaning. 'But you can [tell me its meaning],' he says to Daniel, 'because the spirit of the holy gods is in you' (v.18). The natural man does not need a special revelation from God to inform him that before him lie many trials until the last final humbling and tumbling into the grave. Human experience tells all men of that fact. Death lies before us all, and everyone's philosophy of life should take into consideration life's unavoidable realities. You and I are going to die. What the natural man needs is periodic awakenings to the sobriety of that event. How often does God, through man's conscience and through providence, summon men to the great bar of judgment! Where does hope lie?

On learning of the death of her grandmother, an old Christian friend wrote in a letter to the woman he later married:

How real is death, and how dismal except as its darkness is illumined by the hope of resurrection to life! It is as we look death squarely in the face that the grace and power of the Saviour take on new meaning. How tawdry are all human attempts to dress it up! The light and faith of Jesus alone can cast a halo of joy and hope around it. Blessed are the dead who die in the Lord, and only they! There is nothing that any person can place between himself and the damnation that sin demands, but the merit, blood, righteousness, mediatorship, and intercession of the risen and glorified Redeemer.

A once majestic tree reduced to a stump was a fearful sign, and the sign's interpretation brought to the king fearful words of imminent judgment. Though he was the mightiest man on earth, and could afford the finest physicians and sorcerers in the world, it was sickness and death that lay before him—as before all mankind.

The second striking mercy Nebuchadnezzar receives is *to have that revelation opened up to him by the man of God*. The king sends for Daniel and tells him the entire dream, and Daniel is overwhelmed. He has known the king for some years, and been the beneficiary of his kindnesses. The king had appointed Daniel ruler over the entire province of Babylon, and when he heard this dream he 'was greatly perplexed for a time, and his thoughts terrified him' (v.19)—so much so that the king noticed it and actually reassures him: 'do not let the dream or its meaning alarm you.' Daniel then interprets it with the utmost reluctance. 'If only the dream applied to your enemies!', he muttered, and then, plucking up all his courage, as one standing before the King of kings as well as before this monarch, he says, 'you, O king, are that tree!' (v.22). It is indeed Nebuchadnezzar who is soon to be utterly humiliated, reduced to living with animals, eating grass like a cow, drenched with the dew of the morning, his hair growing like the feathers of an eagle and his nails like the claws of a bird (vv.25, 33). This state would last for an appointed period, just until the time came when the broken and rejected Nebuchadnezzar would humble his heart and 'acknowledge that the Most High is sovereign over the kingdoms of men and gives them to anyone he wishes' (v.25). Yet Daniel did not stop there: 'be pleased to accept my advice,' he said; 'Renounce your sins by doing what is right, and your wickedness by being kind to the oppressed. It may be that then your prosperity will continue' (v.27).

It is a message to Nebuchadnezzar that he would

enjoy a period of tranquillity if he repented. But is there not more in the message than the offer of temporal mercies? Who knows what may happen if a sinner under judgment repents? The city of Nineveh had received a message from the Lord as uncompromisingly bleak as Nebuchadnezzar's: 'Forty more days and Nineveh will be overturned' (Jonah 3:4). But when the word reached the king of Nineveh he rose from his throne, took off his royal robes, covered himself with sackcloth and sat down in the dust. Then he issued a proclamation in Nineveh: 'Let everyone call urgently on God. Let them give up their evil ways and their violence. Who knows? God may yet relent and with compassion turn from his fierce anger so that we will not perish' (Jonah 3:6-9). The men of Nineveh had so little, but used everything they knew of God to escape his judgment.

Babylon was as wicked as Nineveh. There were furnaces into which live men and women were thrown. They practised oppression, slavery, and drunken orgies in the king's palace (5:1). Idolatry was enforced upon the empire. What does one do about such sins? 'Renounce them!' says Daniel, 'And do what is right. Be kind to the oppressed, because judgment is coming upon you.' How courageous young Daniel was to speak to this tyrant in that way! Did the memory of an earlier prophet, Nathan, inspire him? Another king had sinned a great sin, taking another man's wife so that she became pregnant, and then arranging the murder of her brave husband. It was a reprehensible act, and finally Nathan the prophet had gone to that king, saying to David, 'You are the man' worthy of judgment.

The greatest preacher of the English Reformation was Hugh Latimer, and often he was called to preach before King Henry VIII. When he was made a king's chaplain a courtier said to him, 'Beware of contradicting the king. Speak as he speaks, and instead of presuming to lead him, strive to follow him.' 'Away with your counsel!' replied Latimer. He took his calling seriously, and all he read confirmed his need to be faithful. One day he picked up Augustine's writings and read there, 'He who for fear of any power hides the truth, provokes the wrath of God to come upon him, for he fears men more than God.' Another day he picked up Chrysostom's writings and read, 'He is not only a traitor to the truth who openly for truth teaches a lie, but he also who does not pronounce and show the truth he knows.' Latimer said that those two sentences made him afraid, and he vowed, 'I had rather suffer extreme punishment than be a traitor unto the truth.' He met many obstacles in speaking to the king, some even in his own impetuous make-up, but one day he wrote a letter to Henry VIII:

Your Grace, I must show forth such things as I have learned in Scripture, or else deny Jesus Christ. The which denying ought more to be dreaded than the loss of all temporal goods, honour, promotion, fame, prison, slander, hurts, banishment, and all manner of torments and cruelties, yea, and death itself, be it never so shameful and painful . . . There is as great distance between you and me as between God and man; for you are here to me and to all your subjects in God's stead; and so I should quake to speak of your Grace. But as you are a mortal man having in you the corrupt nature of man, so you have no less need of the merits of Christ's passion for your salvation than I and others of your subjects have.

Merle D'Aubigné, *The Reformation in England,*, vol.2, p.42

The king was not offended by the letter and continued to appreciate his chaplain Hugh Latimer. So too Daniel's integrity was respected by Nebuchadnezzar. Thus the second great mercy Nebuchadnezzar experienced was to hear a faithful man of God telling him the truth about his future.

The final mercy from God in this fourth chapter was *the year of grace which Nebuchadnezzar was given* in which to do what Daniel had urged him to do—renounce his sins by doing what was right. Nineveh had only forty days, and their king did not waste a moment, but Nebuchadnezzar was the object of God's long-suffering for a whole year. How often Daniel spoke to him or prayed for him we do not know, but we do know that at the end of that year nothing had changed in Babylon or in the king's life. None of us knows if we have a year left, or even forty days. We cannot guarantee the next forty minutes. The only time we have is this moment. Whatever we know of God we are to use to renounce our sins, do what is right, and call urgently on God. Who knows what doing that will achieve?

Twelve months went by in which Nebuchadnezzar could destroy the torture chambers, send the prisoners home, repent of his wasted life and cast himself upon the mercy of God; but this man did nothing. Then one day, a year after Daniel had spoken to him, he was walking on the roof of his splendid palace under the starry sky, and he looked with pride upon all he surveyed, saying 'Is not this the great Babylon I have built as the royal residence, by my mighty power and for the glory of my majesty?' (v.30). The sentiments accurately reflect Nebuchadnezzar's attitude. He was primarily a builder rather than a warrior, and his own statements, preserved upon cuneiform inscriptions, show his pride in the city and palace which he rebuilt. His words were also a barometer of his heart's condition, desperately arrogant in spite of many warnings. At the sound of those words another voice echoed from heaven implementing the judgment spoken a year earlier (vv.31-33). From that moment on, guided down from the roof with a wild light in his eyes, he was transformed into a virtual animal. If Daniel, the prime minister, were to seek an audience with his king, Nebuchadnezzar the emperor of Babylon, he would be taken to the royal orchard and shown a pathetic figure lying on the ground, wet with dew, his hair like eagle's feathers, glancing up for a moment to see whose shadow this was upon his field before returning to the task of thrusting grass into his mouth with a clawed hand. The dream and its interpretation had been fulfilled. The mighty tree had been cut down. The promised judgment had come as the Most High had decreed. Nebuchadnezzar had learned that he lived in a moral universe, and what he had sowed, that very thing he now reaped.

Those days of divinely administered lycanthropy (the apparent disease from which he was suffering) at last ended. 'Seven times' passed (v.32) and it became 'the end of that time' (v.34). How long that period was we do not know. Some ancient writers consider it to have been for seven years. Among the fragments in Qumran Cave IV (1955) was an Aramaic fragment now called *The Prayer of Nabonidus*. It is regarded as coming from the second half of the first century BC. On this fragment the speaker identifies himself as *Nbny* (probably Nabonidus), king of Assyria and Babylonia, and claims that for seven years he was struck with an evil inflammation. When he confessed his sins, a Jew of the exile explained matters to him. The writer of this fragment, it

51

would seem, has confused matters, attributing to Nabonidus the illness of Nebuchadnezzar. After an allotted period the king's insanity ended, his reason returned to him and he breaks into praising the Most High God in some of the most glorious words exalting God's sovereignty in all of Scripture:

His dominion is an eternal dominion; his kingdom endures from generation to generation. All the peoples of the earth are regarded as nothing. He does as he pleases with the powers of heaven and the peoples of the earth. No-one can hold back his hand or say to him: 'What have you done?' (vv.34-35).

What is this fourth chapter of Daniel? It is a kind of primitive press release. It is an edict issued by king Nebuchadnezzar from his royal palace, written with the purpose of assuring the worried citizens of Babylon that they are not being ruled by a crazy man. The country had buzzed with rumours of the extraordinary things said to have happened to Nebuchadnezzar. One presumes that Daniel has been guiding the empire during these years. But the day comes when the light of reason again flickers in Nebuchnezzar and the king's health is restored. Then it is that the contents of this chapter are composed, when Nebuchadnezzar issues this statement: 'To the peoples, nations and men of every language, who live in all the world: May you prosper greatly! It is my pleasure to tell you about the miraculous signs and wonders that the Most High God has performed for me . . .' (vv.1-2). And all that follows in this narrative of the decline, fall and renewal of the king is written and preserved in the archives of the Babylonian nation. That is why Daniel recorded them in his book. Everywhere in Babylon God's people gathered around the Word, taught their children, met together, sang the psalms, and looked with hope for a return yet to the land of Israel. They did so under the protection of this chapter, because of all that had happened in the humbling of Nebuchadnezzar.

The chapter reads like the edict of a religious man, but one still muddled in his beliefs. Consider how Daniel is referred to as 'Belteshazzar, after the name of my god, and the spirit of the holy gods is in him' (vv.8, 18). Daniel is also called the 'chief of the magicians' (v.9) The syncretistic language reflects a paganism influenced by the theocratic convictions of Daniel. Though the God of Daniel has been dealing with him in such extraordinary ways, Nebuchadnezzar still thinks in terms of a sort of parliament of gods, a United Nations of deities in heaven, where Israel has its god and Babylon has its god. But the top god, the king has come to recognise, is Daniel's god—'the Most High God' (v.2). Even with all the privileges he has had, and the fearful judgments that have come into his life, Nebuchadnezzar is a confused man. In spite of the transparent life that young Daniel has lived before him as a living word, showing such integrity in all his dealings, even so the king has not even become a monotheist. 'Hear, O Nebuchadnezzar, the Lord God of Daniel is one God.'

The king had heard and seen so much. What signs he had witnessed! Men say, if only they could see a miracle such as a man thrown into a furnace of fire and not being destroyed, then they would believe. But Nebuchadnezzar saw that and did not believe. Or, if men could see the Son of God with their own eyes, then they would become believers. But Nebuchadnezzar had seen him, as the people of Jerusalem were to do—and yet the mob went on to cry, 'Crucify him! Crucify him!' It takes more than signs and wonders to form power evangelism, and even more than a godly life faithfully declaring the Word of God. Let us have that at least, but for a sinner to become a believer it takes regeneration by the sovereign Spirit. It takes the obedience of faith in those things we have received from the Most High God. It takes accepting the advice of the Word of God, 'Renounce your sins by doing what is right', and crying mightily to Christ to save. It takes a person saying,

> The dearest idol I have known,
> Whate'er that idol be,
> Help me to tear it from Thy throne,
> And worship only Thee.
> (William Cowper, 1731–1800)

Nebuchadnezzar's life demonstrates the truth of Jesus' own words, 'How hard it is for the rich to enter the kingdom of God!' (Luke 18:24).

54

2
Under Belshazzar
Daniel, the forgotten man

Between the royal edict of Nebuchadnezzar in chapter 4 and the first year of the reign of king Belshazzar (5:1) there was a period of thirty years. Little is known of this period, and there is nothing to encourage us to believe that Nebuchadnezzar had come to a knowledge of Daniel's Lord. For example, while with the aid of his wife Amytis Nebuchadnezzar spent these years in the embellishment of his capital, he also improved the temples of Marduk and Nabu, establishing many shrines in Babylon for these gods and providing regular offerings for them. He also restored temples in Sippar, Marad, and Borsippa. These are hardly the actions of a man who has learned from his encounters with God.

Fifty years have passed since Daniel was taken as a small boy from Israel. Belshazzar was in fact the grandson of Nebuchadnezzar. His father was named Nabonidus, and he had entrusted the army and the kingship to Belshazzar while he campaigned in central Arabia, where he eventually remained for ten years. The real authority in the nation lay with the queen, Belshazzar's mother. Daniel has fallen into disfavour, living in Babylon largely as a forgotten man. Belshazzar has not even heard of this man who is the spokesman of the living God. The bearer of God's truth has been marginalised, and life goes on at the hub of the Babylonian empire without any of the influence of the Word of God.

The Bible presents us with two developments in the history of the world. First, it tells us that the kingdom of God will spread and grow like a mustard seed that becomes a great tree (Matthew 13:31-32); the nations will come like birds to the tree and find their homes in its branches. Again (v.33), God's kingdom is like yeast or leaven that permeates a mass of dough. The climactic picture of this is described by the apostle Paul in Romans 11—a time for the future fullness of Israel and then great riches for the Gentiles. A time is coming when the acceptance of Israel into the favour and blessing of God will mean life from the dead for the rest of the world (vv.12, 15). That is one picture in Scripture.

There is another theme in Scripture, and that is of wickedness, vital and relentless, which goes on until the end. Multitudes continue to find the broad road to destruction and only few find the way to life (Matthew 7:13-14). People in the shadow of the end of the ages will be behaving no better than people did when Noah's flood cascaded over the world (Matthew 24:38-39). The climactic picture for that is found in 2 Thessalonians 2:3-12, which tells of the 'man of sin' (or 'lawlessness') who is going to be revealed, and a great rebellion against God taking place, perhaps fuelled by a backlash against the renewed vitality of the gospel and the great riches which the Gentiles have received.

So there are these two contrasting but not incompatible perspectives, two kingdoms at war, and at times one seems to gain the ascendancy and then the other, with the ultimate denouement at the end of all things before the coming of the Lord Christ.

1. The dream in the first year of Belshazzar (Daniel 7)

Daniel 7 tells us that in the first year of Belshazzar, who came to the throne about 556 BC, the prophet himself had a dream. Daniel had interpreted the dreams of others, but now God speaks to *him* in this way. The dream presented to him—and to ourselves—an outline of the course of history. God has a blueprint for his creation, and according to that plan he works all things, from the greatest to the least, after the counsel of his own will (Ephesians 1:11). There are some secret things which God hides from men, and there are others which he reveals (Deuteronomy 29:29). He may communicate by a dream or vision. He calls his prophets into his presence and speaks to them, and they come forth with a message which they prefix with the words, 'Thus saith the Lord'. Daniel, like the other writing prophets, 'wrote down the substance of the dream' (v.1). Daniel did not explain every one of the details, even if he could have understood them all. We are not told the meaning of each constituent element, but we are given the big picture.

Daniel sees first 'the great sea' (v.2) and it is being lashed by winds from all directions, foaming, threatening and restless. This sea is a picture of the nations of the world, and there is never a calm—consider the continent of Africa, South America, the Middle East, Ulster and the Balkans. Then Daniel, as he watches the tumultuous sea, sees four beasts emerging from its depths one after the other. These great monsters rise up and for a while straddle the history of the world; then they simply disappear and others succeed them. Who are they? 'The four great beasts are four kingdoms that will rise from the earth' (v.17).

Powers today are represented by symbols of beasts—the Russian bear, the American eagle, the Chinese dragon. Daniel saw four beasts: a lion (v.4), a bear (v.5), a leopard (v.6), and then one so horrible that Daniel did not know what to call it (v.7). The sea does not represent any particular geographical area of water, but the vast limitless deep. But the beasts represent specific human kingdoms, and though they have particular application to Daniel's time there is the bigger picture, that in world history one kingdom briefly succeeds another as top dog. Forces of extraordinary power and cruelty energise themselves, and for a while cast a shadow across the world. One will follow another until the ultimate one will be struck down by the breath of Christ's mouth.

In *The Times* this year (10 April 1997) there was a review of a book entitled *The Scarlet Memorial: Tales of Cannibalism in Modern China*. Over 100,000 people in the first years of the Cultural Revolution were murdered in China, and actual cannibalism re-emerged. The author of this book is Zheng Yi, a former Red Guard. How could such horrors have happened? Zheng Yi says, ' . . . we attempted to bring about a beautiful society. We thought that after treading through the quagmire of blood . . . we would be able to face the most magnificent dawn in the history of mankind. Instead we consorted with beasts.' Even more recently, *The Times* reviewed a book on the subject of the reappearance of Fascism in Europe in the last decade of the twentieth century (8 August 1997). That book has the significant title *The Beast Reawakens*. That image of the rise of beasts is the picture Daniel gives us here; rulers emerge who act in a subhuman way and with absolute power. This hideous century, now drawing to a close, has witnessed

58

the greatest display since the fall of Adam of such beasts waxing and waning.

We recall that Nebuchadnezzar had had a dream in which the great figure of a man dominated everything. Its theme was the triumph of mankind's culture, achievements and beauty. The king saw a statue, and the words that are used to describe it in Scripture are 'an enormous, dazzling statue, awesome in appearance' (2:31). Nebuchadnezzar was dreaming of the same subject that Daniel dreams of in chapter 7—world history. But what Nebuchadnezzar sees are the glories of man, his formidable achievements, what men can construct of gold, silver, bronze, iron and clay. We think of ancient Greece's splendours, Rome under the Caesars, the sixteenth-century Renaissance, Venice and Genoa under its doges, Paris under Louis XIV and, today, the island of Manhattan. Consider what man has built: his universities, hospitals, space rockets and stations, satellites and the World Wide Web. Think of what man has created: his music, literature, art, architecture—all the glittering achievements of man—just like the golden figure of which Nebuchadnezzar dreamed, and of which men dream may yet emerge in the new millennium.

When Daniel the man of God dreams, his dream is of the very same subject, the history of the world; but he does not see a man, he dreams of wild beasts. Not creations of high culture, but creatures that live to get the mastery, put down any opposition, and destroy. Daniel, with the Spirit of Christ in him, could never dream like Nebuchadnezzar as both looked on the world. When he was awake, Daniel could look through his windows and survey the real glories of Babylon, just as the devil showed Christ 'all the kingdoms of the

59

world and their splendour' (Matthew 4:8). But when God shows him the world of humanity, he sees ferocious animals—a roaring lion, a hungry bear, a swift leopard, an unknown beast. We live our lives with that same tension. When we think of Rome we think of the majestic Coliseum, but we also think of Nero and the beastly cruelties within that awesome edifice. When we look at Manhattan's skyscrapers they can take our breath away, but we also see in their shadow mammon, greed, drugs, sensuality and abuse. From one perspective the history of man is the story of extraordinary achievements, and then from another perspective it is a decadent, depraved and bestial chronicle. The Word of God is saying, 'You remember how Nebuchadnezzar had seen the history of mankind? Now let me also show you this: great nations will devour small nations; the god of this world will always be at war with the saints of the Most High. The world system is ultimately anti-Christian. Its great power structures are like wild beasts that stalk the lambs of Christ's flock. I am sending you forth as sheep amidst wolves.'

So these four beasts symbolise the power structures raised by men, and for Daniel and his first readers they were a succession of empires that were immediately recognisable. They also have a trans-historical significance, representing that succession of world-dominant powers that rise and fall from Daniel's time until the end. There is virtually no power of man that is not symbolised in the emergence and the swift disappearance of these creatures.

The first is the lion, and it corresponds with the head of gold in Nebuchadnezzar's image The symbolism of the lion and eagles' wings speaks eloquently of Babylon (cf. Jeremiah 4:7; 49:19). The lion is the king of the beasts,

and with its outstretched wings it is a fine symbol of
Babylon whose influence spread over all the surround-
ing nations, even Jerusalem and Israel. But Daniel sees
the wings torn off so that the power of Babylon is limit-
ed, and it is cut down to size 'so that it stood on two
feet like a man' (v.4). A foretaste of this happened to
Nebuchadnezzar in his madness, and it will happen to
Babylon itself. Empires rise, they have their moment of
glory, and they are humbled. However much the
tyrants boast of their invincibility, down they fall. Only
God's kingdom endures. The dream is saying, 'Do not
be intimidated. The greatest powers of the earth are
transitory beasts.'

> And though they take our life,
> Goods, honour, children, wife,
> Yet is their profit small:
> These things shall vanish all;
> The city of God remaineth.
>
> (Martin Luther, 1483–1546;
> tr. by Thomas Carlyle, 1795–1881)

The second beast is a bear (v.5) who has been
devouring its prey, and there are three ribs still sticking
out of his mouth. He has gorged himself on carrion,
and yet is raised up on one side, preparing to leap. He
is hungry for slaughter and is being urged on by someone crying to him, 'Get up and eat your fill of flesh!'
(v.5). If the lion is Babylon, then the bear probably represents the Medes and Persians with their appetite for
expansion. Aggrandisement is the characteristic of
every nation, because it is the characteristic of fallen
man. Every nation, even little Switzerland, Luxem-
bourg and Liechtenstein, is hungry for wealth. The

world's bankers become bears. Given the opportunity, every single nation would become a bear. The poorest nations test-explode nuclear bombs. Their statesmen say they are non-aligned, the descendants of Ghandi, and that they love peace; yet India has the fourth largest army in the whole world. Peace-loving little Ireland is full of bears as its island has become known for internecine strife and thousands have been killed. Nations everywhere seize any opportunity of expanding their borders, retaliating, stockpiling weapons, encouraging economic aggression, heeding that mysterious voice crying to them, 'Get up, get up, eat your fill of flesh!' That is the spirit of a rebel world.

The third beast is a leopard. It has four heads, and it has four wings 'like those of a bird'. Historically, after Babylon, and then the Medes and the Persians, Greece arose as swiftly as Alexander's conquests themselves. The young king struck like lightning; his troops were so mobile that he turned his armies around from one nation to fall upon another within a matter of weeks. After he died his kingdom was divided into four. But the chief meaning of these four heads is to symbolise the universal expansion of this third kingdom out into the four corners of the earth (2:39). Daniel is observing things happening at greater speed. The cumbersome bear has become this swift panther. The process of self-exaltation and self-gratification becomes instant. But what is the rapidity of Alexander the Great's military might compared to today's push of a red button with its potential for destroying continents?

Then there is the fourth beast (v.7), but this one is not identified by Daniel. It must be a symbol of the historical Roman Empire, but given special significance as the power that put to death the Messiah and violently ended the covenant relationship of Jerusalem with Jehovah. It is antichrist in a way the preceding beasts were not. It is nondescript, yet introduced with particular solemnity. No likeness can be found for it in all the vast animal kingdom. This beast has extraordinary power. It is grotesque and terrifying, half-animal and half-machine. We are told that it has large 'iron teeth and bronze claws' (v.19) and it devours everything in its path. It has ten horns, and one of them has 'eyes like the eyes of a man and a mouth that spoke boastfully' (v.8). It is some fearful, genetically engineered combination of animal and human and machine. This beast is merciless even to itself, for it can turn and uproot three of its own horns (v.8). 'It was different from all the former beasts' (v.7), principally because it declares war on the people of God (v.21). This human development in technology is put to work in a war between the kingdoms of this world and the kingdom of God. Daniel longs to know 'the true meaning of the fourth beast' (v.19). For him it is the final beast to appear after a succession of persecuting powers that have come into the world. This beast is also singled out as having ten horns upon its head, and for the presence of a little horn (vv.7-8). So there are kingdoms that will exist during a prolonged second phase of the beast's history. They will not necessarily arise immediately after the downfall of Rome, but they can trace their lineage back to Rome. Then a little horn will emerge, and this stands for a man, a government, a coalition of governments or even an ideology. Whatever the little horn is, he opposes the saints until the judgment of God brings about the complete destruction of this final beast (v.11).

The New Testament speaks of the 'coming of the lawless one which will be in accordance with the work of Satan displayed in all kinds of counterfeit miracles, signs and wonders and in every sort of evil that deceives' (2 Thessalonians 2:9-10). The only event after his appearing will be the coming of the Son of Man. Daniel is told that this beast will 'try to change the set times and the laws' (v.25). He seeks to control world events, and rule providence itself: 'he sets himself up in God's temple, proclaiming himself to be God' (2 Thessalonians 2:4). Speaking of this in Matthew 24:22, Jesus tells of the great distress prefigured in the destruction of Jerusalem with the ending of God's covenant with the land of Israel, which time of tribulation is one day to be repeated, but with more intense fierceness, so that it seems impossible for those who love God to survive. Then, Daniel says, the end is at hand: 'the Ancient of Days came and pronounced judgment in favour of the saints of the Most High, and the time came when they possessed the kingdom' (v.22). That cruel time will be cut short, the Lord Jesus promises. He will not allow the turtle-dove to be torn in pieces by the wild beasts. The Good Shepherd will save his sheep from being destroyed.

Daniel's dream presents us with the backcloth for these two and a half thousand years against which the church of God so far has sought to love and serve the Lord Jesus Christ in this world. She has lived her life before the beasts, and always must. The people of God have a commission to be always abounding in the work of the Lord, and in that work they cry out at times, 'Save me from the lion's mouth' (Psalm 22:21). They want to annexe principalities and communities and bring them into the true kingdom. They respect no boundaries. They will not be intimidated by any power structures. They must obey God rather than man.

Giving in to weariness is for them to sign their own death warrant. Their growth is the condition of their survival. Their obedience to their King's great commission is the mark of being true subjects. What is the determination of a beast compared to theirs in bringing all the world under the Saviour's rule? All the world must bow to King Jesus. Without iron teeth and bronze claws, they have a mouth full of good things and stretch out their hands all day long to a disobedient people. Such weapons as these are mighty through God to the pulling down of strongholds.

That is the dream and the interpretation of the four beasts. Then Daniel sees something else of far greater significance, a mighty throne (vv.9ff.). He must not be distracted by the remorseless procession of beasts so as to fail to look at what is set high above the beasts and the sea. It is from this throne that these monsters are being controlled. All the time Daniel gazes at this new sight, he can hear the distraction in the background of the mouth of the little horn speaking boastfully (vv.8, 11). But 'the Ancient of Days' is seated upon the throne: that is, God seen as mature as the universe itself, with all the wisdom of its Creator reigning over everything. From this throne he is head over all things—including those beasts—to the church. He is like a divine lion-tamer—when he gives permission the beasts may emerge from the ocean's depths. When Daniel takes his eyes off that throne the world itself is in a state of turbulence; but let him look up and there is the glorious peace of an unshakeable throne.

Daniel has the difficulty of any creature in describing the figure of God, so he uses these images of white, dazzling white clothing and hair, a throne flaming with fire, wheels ablaze, rivers of fire, and all the time thousands upon thousands, and ten thousand times ten thousand, standing before him, all looking to God, waiting for him to give the decree and moving at his bidding.

> Thousands of thousands stand around
>   Thy throne, O God most high;
> Ten thousand times ten thousand sound
>   Thy praise; but who am I?
>
> (John Mason, c. 1646–94)

Finally, he comes, while the last beast has risen from the sea:

one like a son of man, coming with the clouds of heaven. He approached the Ancient of Days and was led into his presence. He was given authority, glory and sovereign power; all peoples, nations and men of every language worshipped him. His dominion is an everlasting dominion that will not pass away, and his kingdom is one that will never be destroyed (vv.13-14).

The beasts have a Judge to whom they must give account. The greatest of them can do nothing without his decree, and he also must answer to this 'son of man'. It was this vision that our Lord had in mind when he referred to himself before the high priest and the court of the Sanhedrin as the Son of Man (Matthew 26:64). In the heart of the Old Testament this vision of the sovereignty of the Lord Jesus Christ is given. All things are of him, and all things are to him. The command comes from him, even for the times of persecution to arise and the church to be hunted like a partridge in the wilderness.

66

Sovereign Ruler of the skies,
Ever gracious ever wise;
All my times are in Thy hand,
All events at Thy command.

Plagues and deaths around me fly;
Till he bids, I cannot die;
Not a single shaft can hit,
Till the God of love sees fit.

(John Ryland, 1753-1825)

He does according to his will amongst that innumerable company in heaven, yes, but the beasts too must do what he bids. The greatest events in world history are to be judged by him, yes, and the smallest things too, every idle word evaluated by him, with nothing overlooked. We must all stand before this great throne, and sitting upon it will be this Son of Man. All our comfort in that great day will derive from one fact, that the one who died to be our Saviour is sitting upon that throne. The one who will vindicate us is the Lamb who on Golgotha bore our sins. The beasts have no choice in obeying him. For them the yoke is not easy nor the burden light. They too must give account when they will bow before him. But his people cry with longing, *Maranatha*—'Even so, come, Lord Jesus' (Revelation 22:20 AV). It is this message that comes to Daniel at a time when the Word of God seems to have been consigned to oblivion in Babylon: 'The Sovereignty lies with the Lord.'

2 A ram and a goat (Daniel 8)

Though this dream of the beasts and the throne comes

to Daniel, nothing happens for two long years. Belshazzar is still on the throne and Daniel is the forgotten man of Babylon. In chapter 8 we are informed that in the third year of king Belshazzar Daniel has a vision of a fight between two animals—a ram and a goat. The ram has two powerful horns, one bigger than the other (v.3), and he charges toward the west and the north and the south. Evidently the ram comes from the east, and it appears irresistible—'no animal could stand against him, and none could rescue from his power. He did as he pleased and became great' (v.4). What is the ram? We do not need to speculate because a messenger from God, whose appearance was like a man's and whose name was Gabriel (vv.15-16), tells Daniel that the ram with the two horns 'represents the kings of Media and Persia' (v.20).

Then in the vision Daniel sees a goat coming from the west, travelling so fast that, like a hovercraft, he skims the surface of the ground (v.5). The goat smashes into the ram 'in great rage' (v.6) and shatters both his horns. Whereas we had been told, 'No animal could stand against the ram' (v.4), now we see that the ram itself was powerless to stand against the goat. Daniel is also told the identity of the goat. 'The shaggy goat is the king of Greece, and the large horn between his eyes is the first king' (v.21): that is, this horn represents Alexander the Great, who conquered the whole of the Middle East by the time he was 30 years of age, and died grieving that there were no more conquests to be made. 'The goat became very great, but at the height of his power his large horn was broken off' (v.8). Alexander's kingdom was broken into four smaller kingdoms, Macedonia, Thrace, Syria and Egypt, and so this prophecy was fulfilled: 'in its place four prominent horns grew up toward the four winds of heaven' (v.8). Again we are being shown the history of mankind—the clashing of the brittle horns—one nation overcoming another which a short time earlier had seemed virtually impregnable. When the smoke of battle blows away, not a beast survives and not even a horn is intact. The price of victory is as costly as the price of defeat.

The war between ram and goat is simply the background for the heart of Daniel 8, which is a warning of another horn of exceptional malice. This horn is described in two sections (vv.9-12 & 23-25) and is not intended to be identified with the little horn of chapter 7. The horn of chapter 8 is expressly identified as a king who shall arise from Greece (not from Rome as the horn of chapter 7), and the various characteristics of this horn reveal how dissimilar it is in origin, nature and destiny. So out of one of the four prominent horns, that is, from one of the four kingdoms into which Alexander's empire was broken, comes another horn (v.9). Its smallness is not emphasised, merely the fact that it 'started small but grew in power' (v.9).

This horn which 'grew in power to the south and the east and towards the Beautiful Land' (v.9) is known to be a specific king, whose name was Antiochus Epiphanes IV. Information is given about him in this chapter so that the earlier readers of Daniel would be forewarned of his rise. He came from one of the divisions of the former empire of Alexander. He started insignificantly enough, of the most humble origins, but rose in power because of a single-minded ruthlessness. It was in the year 175 BC that he began his infamous reign. One looks in vain for some noble qualities to explain how he achieved such significance. We are told about him that he was 'a stern-faced king, a master of intrigue' (v.23). He became powerful by giving favour to any who would betray their friends and allies, and to men who had no scruples. When he got to the top he still behaved as if he were living in the underworld. Daniel is warned, 'He will become very strong, but not by his own power. He will cause astounding devastation and succeed in whatever he does' (v.24). On coins in the latter part of his reign he actually called himself (Theos) Epiphanes—'(god) manifest'. The horn reached for the stars (v.10), claiming equality with God. A day came when Antiochus Epiphanes focused his attention on Israel 'the Beautiful Land' (v.9), and on its 'mighty men and the holy people' (v.24). It was in the year 169 BC that he first entered the temple in Jerusalem. He insisted on going into the Holy of Holies, and carried off some of the gold and silver vessels. He further determined to Hellenise Palestine: that is, to dismantle the whole of the worship of the Lord. A religious persecution of unprecedented bitterness commenced. Sabbath-keeping and the practice of circumcision were forbidden under pain of death; sacrifices in the temple were outlawed, and prostitution was established there. The people of God who loved the Word were subjected to every kind of degradation and brutality. On 25 December 167 BC a Greek altar was erected on the site of the old one; this was the last straw and led to the Maccabean revolt. Daniel's vision describes Antiochus's activities in somewhat mysterious language: the horn 'set itself up to be as great as the Prince of the host; it took away the daily sacrifice from him, and the place of the sanctuary was brought low. Because of rebellion, the host of the saints and the daily sacrifice were given over to it. It prospered in everything it did, and truth was thrown to the ground' (vv.11-12). It was all so abominable that it made the hearts of the people of God desolate to hear of the desecration done to their Lord and his temple. All this took place in Jerusalem between the years 171 and 165 BC. It lasted 2300 long evenings and mornings (v.14), almost seven years, and then the sanctuary was restored.

In the dream recorded in chapter 7 Daniel had already seen a shadowy figure emerging at the end of human history, in Satan's last desperate attempt to lead the world's rebellion against God. That man will attempt to dethrone God and scatter the hosts of heaven. In fact, the apostle Paul echoes the language of Daniel 8 to describe the final appearing of the man of sin: 'He will oppose and will exalt himself over everything that is called God or is worshipped, so that he sets himself up in God's temple, proclaiming himself to be God' (2 Thessalonians 2:4). In this chapter Daniel is being shown that the horn that grows in power 'until it reached the host of the heavens' (v.10) is somehow also a more ominous figure than one Greek king. That same spirit that possessed Antiochus, and allowed him to achieve his earthly success 'not by his own power' (v.24), will energise the final man of lawlessness at the end of the age. As Ronald S. Wallace writes:

When the people of God in the second century before Christ were made the target of this earthly ruler's spite and cunning, they were suffering under a hatred far more intense, deceitful and determined than is the normal fate of a historically enslaved people. They were indeed suffering as the immediate and ready target of the powers of evil that hate God's work and are out to destroy for ever whatever confesses his name. They were being attacked by a typical

71

Antichrist even before Christ came in the flesh! Daniel was thus able to attach a unique importance to this little figure, Antiochus Epiphanes, arising so dramatically out of the Greek dynasty, whose career had such a baneful effect on the life of the people of God that he could dominate their official rulers, desecrate their sanctuary and cause even sacrifice to cease—he was a sign and symbol of what is to come at the end.   (*The Lord is King*, IVP, p.145)

So it is the rise of this figure, to which Daniel will return again in his book, which is at the heart of the vision described for us in chapter 8.

The normal Puritan structure of a sermon ended with a climactic section entitled 'Uses', which consisted of the application of the passage to the hearers. There are at least five 'uses' for application of the last couple of verses in this chapter.

1. The first use comes from the fact that *all the above is true* (v.26). This vision with its interpretation is not a fantasy. The goat destroyed the ram and then himself perished, his large horn being broken off at the height of his power, and in its place grew four prominent horns. Out of one of them came another horn, who was Antiochus Epiphanes. All this *did* occur; it is true. The Lord Jesus Christ said of God's Scriptures, 'Your word is truth' (John 17:17). That is the only rationale for such an event as this—hundreds of people spending a week of their annual vacation in a Christian conference, where the climax of each day is to gather around a book in the Bible that was written 2500 years ago, hearing it expounded and applied to their own daily living. Why should people use their time thus? The only answer to

72

that question is that these words are true. Many reasons are suggested why people should become Christians: the strength it will give to human relationships; the peace it will give at death; the grace to handle moral and emotional problems that come into our lives. All those are good reasons for becoming Christians, but ultimately there is only one reason why anyone should become a Christian. It is because the Christian faith is true. We study the Bible to obey it because it is true. That is the first use.

2. The second use is found in the words of God to Daniel, when he tells him that this mighty anti-Christian figure will be destroyed 'not by human power' (v.25)—that is, not by assassination with the sword or defeat in battle. *The time will come for God himself to act.* It is a spine-tingling experience to hear a great Dutch congregation sing Essenburg's transcription of Psalm 68:

> God shall arise and by his might
> Put all his enemies to flight
>   With shame and consternation.
> His haters, haughty though they be,
> Shall at his august presence flee
>   In utter desolation.
> For when Jehovah shall appear,
> He shall consume, afar and near,
>   All those that evil cherish.
> As smoke before His dreadful ire,
> As wax is melted by the fire,
>   So shall the wicked perish.

So one day, on a campaign in Media in 164 BC Antiochus

Epiphanes was overwhelmed by an attack of pain. There was a brief mysterious illness—a form of dementia—and he was a dead man. His little journey from the womb to the tomb was all over. As Luther sang,

> And let the prince of ill
> Look grim as e'er he will,
> He harms us not a whit;
> For why? his doom is writ;
> A word shall quickly slay him.

3. The third use is found in what Gabriel tells Daniel: 'seal up the vision' (v.26)—that is, *keep it safe*; preserve it safely. It is going to be fulfilled. The people of God after Daniel's day were going to need this Word, so it must be guarded well. Every householder has certain documents which do not merely lie around on the table like junk mail. They are too important for that. Some are even placed in safe-deposit boxes: others are locked in drawers. Everyone is careful with certificates, deeds and wills. The church has been given by her Master the Word of God. How do we keep it safe? By knowing what it says, hiding it in our hearts, giving it the unquestioned place of centrality in our congregations, treating it as authoritative about everything on which it pronounces. Has much of the professing church done that? Has it not rather put it alongside other documents—the alleged 'assured results of modern criticism', the books of psychiatry, handbooks of sketches and dramas, the scientific manuals on human origins, and New Age meditations on 'spirituality'? Has it not lost the revealed 'vision' in the clutter of many other conflicting voices? Seal up the vision, Daniel is told.

4. The fourth use is what we are told of Daniel's response to this vision. He was utterly 'exhausted and lay ill for several days' (v.27a). The great Word of God had come to him with the Holy Ghost sent down from heaven, and Daniel wasn't jumping and laughing; *he was thoroughly overwhelmed* and 'appalled by the vision; it was beyond understanding' (v.27c). When the people listened to the apostle Peter's word to them at the feast of Pentecost they were cut to their hearts at what they heard (Acts 2:37). We pray for a religious awakening, and so we must. We long for the gospel to come not in word only, but with power and with the Holy Spirit and with much assurance (1 Thessalonians 1:5). Yet how demanding that can be upon those whose burden and gift it is to take that Word to the world, as well as to those who hear them! Think of the evangelist George Whitefield, the day before he died while yet in his mid-fifties. Someone said to him, 'Sir, you are more fit to go to bed than to preach.' 'True, Sir,' he said, and then, clasping his hands together, he prayed, 'Lord Jesus, I am weary in thy work, but not of thy work. If I have not yet finished my course, let me go and speak for thee once more in the fields, seal thy truth, and come home and die.' Within hours Whitefield was dead. For Jeremiah the word of revelation that came to him was as a fire burning in his bones. If he would not speak it would still burn, but if he spoke there would be other burnings. There could be no escape from the fires.

5. The fifth use is seen in the prophet's response to the vision. What did Daniel do? 'Then I got up and went about the king's business' (v.27b). That is, *he went about his lawful calling and did his duty day by day*. The king might have no awareness at all of his existence, but

Daniel knew his duty. That is a great word to every one of us. One Sunday we were in church, and this mighty shattering Word of God came to us. It so overwhelmed us that we almost felt destroyed by what we saw of the plight of man and our own guilt. Our only hope lay in this mighty God, his Son Jesus Christ and what he had done for sinners. Then on Monday morning we got up and went about our employer's business. We did it with that word still burning in our lives, but as new men doing the old work. Paul writes to slaves living in revival times and tells them, 'Slaves, obey your earthly masters in everything; and do it, not only when their eye is on you and to win their favour, but with sincerity of heart and reverence for the Lord. Whatever you do, work at it with all your heart, as working for the Lord, not for men' (Colossians 3:22-23).

3. Belshazzar's feast and the writing on the wall (Daniel 5)

These long silent years go by in which Daniel appears to be sidelined, but God had not given the gift of leadership and prophecy to this man in vain. God never gives graces to his servants for them to atrophy. We need his gifts to stand and wait. Remember the forty years Moses spent in 'the backside of the desert'. The years of patience require the gift of faith, and all this time the Lord is strengthening Daniel, preparing him for the imminent confrontation with Belshazzar and his coming in from the cold to be entrusted with those crucial years of national leadership and yet of trial under King Darius. Daniel is learning that the Sovereign Lord controls every period of our own personal histories.

In chapter 5 the story of Daniel moves on a further

fourteen years. It is the last year of Belshazzar's reign, though the king is not aware of that. In fact, it is the last night of Belshazzar's life. It is a fearful fact that many come to their last hours without being aware of it or being prepared for that certainty. Belshazzar's father Nabonidus is leading his troops into battle not far from the city. He is fighting the Medes and the Persians under Cyrus and Darius, and defeat is staring Nabonidus in the face. We have a window opened in Daniel 5 on what was happening that night in the royal palace. We are shown a drunken feast; Belshazzar is not where a king should be, encouraging the morale of his troops the night before the decisive battle. There was another king who stayed at home in the royal palace and wandered on the roof of his palace while his troops were fighting. That king was David, and the sin and death that came into his life because he was not in the place of duty has sullied his reputation ever since.

This was a particularly great feast, to which a thousand had been invited. The custom at oriental feasts was for the king to sit on a raised platform, apart from the guests. Babylon's feasts were always in the name of some god, and as Belshazzar and his cronies drank they cried one toast after another to every one of their gods (they didn't want to offend any by omitting them): 'As they drank the wine, they praised the gods of gold and silver, of bronze, iron, wood and stone' (v.4). As they became increasingly drunk, Belshazzar gave the order 'to bring in the gold and silver goblets that Nebuchadnezzar his father had taken from the temple in Jerusalem' (v.2). These were the silver cups that caught the blood from the necks of the lambs that were sacrificed for the sins of the people. While they were drunkenly toasting their gods from these vessels, 'Suddenly the fingers of a human hand appeared and wrote on the plaster of the wall, near the lampstand in the royal palace' (v.5). Sometimes you hear some doggerel about God not having any hands but our hands, any feet but our feet, and any voice but our voice, and so on. Yet consider how suddenly the fingers of a human hand appeared and wrote a message to these revellers! Not a Christian was in that room, but the hand of God moved and affected them all. The Lord can after midnight summarily summon a sinner's conscience to stand before his bar of judgment to give an account for his life. In the experience of those who are far from God the hours of darkness are shattered by an inner voice which speaks to them. A few words written by a man is all God needs. Some words from God on a wayside pulpit are enough and its effect can be absolutely devastating: 'The king watched the hand as it wrote. His face turned pale and he was so frightened that his knees knocked together and his legs gave way' (v.6). The smallest action of Almighty God inscribing four words on a wall can mean that nothing is the same again. When Luther saw five words, 'the just live by faith', biblical Christianity was rediscovered and the Reformation was born—the greatest revival since the days of the apostles. What may the living God do with a few words! Augustine of Hippo heard the three words 'Take and read!' chanted by a child, and he went to the Scriptures and read from the letter to the Romans. How many words do we hear week after week? Do they make us tremble? Have we grown too familiar with the Word of God? So many excrescences introduced into modern worship suggest that many are wearied by the Word.

When God was to speak to Belshazzar it was about his sin: 'You have set yourself up against the Lord of heaven . . . you did not honour the God who holds in his hand your life and all your ways' (v.23). It was the first time for God to speak personally to him, and when he did so it was on the night before he died. God came to Belshazzar to speak of his sins of omission—what the king had failed to do. He had the achievements of despotic power reverently recorded in cuneiform tablets, but he had not honoured the living God. He had not lived for God's glory. He was a drunk, but for Belshazzar and his cronies the party was over. God's long-suffering was ending and he came to him one last time giving him this marvellous opportunity—what every worldling in Wales dreams of—and Belshazzar got it! To live like a lord all your life, and then on your very last day to have the opportunity to repent and to seek forgiveness from God for ignoring him for so long! It sounds so wonderful to the unbeliever—and every unregenerate heart says 'That's for me!'

Here is this archetypal sinner, Belshazzar, and the Word of God comes to him, but there are problems. The first is that Belshazzar does not understand it. It is foolishness to him. He is a natural man and he does not know it. He does not recognise the message when it comes to him. 'The man without the Spirit does not accept the things that come from the Spirit of God, for they are foolishness to him, and he cannot understand them, because they are spiritually discerned' (1 Corinthians 2:14). Have you considered the possibility that if there were an occasion in the distant future when God may choose to speak to you, you will not understand a word of what he is saying to you? There was no one around Belshazzar who could explain the Word of God to him. He had never had much time for religious folks and so he had to ask his lackeys. 'The king called out for the enchanters, astrologers, and diviners to be brought' (v.7). So into this night-club atmosphere all his wise men came to explain to him the Word of God. But they could not help him. The Word was as much a mystery to them as to the king. Not one single person in all that vast assembly—the very cream of Babylon—could explain the Word of God to Belshazzar, though he offered them unimaginable authority and riches (v.7)—to be the third highest ruler after Nabonidus and himself.

Then the power behind the throne discovered that the end of feasting had come. The queen mother 'hearing the voices . . . came into the banquet hall' (v.10), to see Belshazzar even more terrified and his nobles baffled. She addresses Belshazzar respectfully:

> O king, live for ever! . . . Don't be alarmed! Don't look so pale! There is a man in your kingdom who has the spirit of the holy gods in him. In the time of your father he was found to have insight and intelligence and wisdom like that of the gods . . . Call for Daniel, and he will tell you what the writing means (vv.10-12).

The queen reminds Belshazzar of his 'father' Nebuchadnezzar. It is the honorary title of a highly respected ancestor, and she refers three times to that fact in one sentence (v.11). Daniel was the man that Belshazzar's 'father' Nebuchadnezzar turned to: Belshazzar could do worse. The queen was not herself a believer; she was obviously a polytheist, believing in the existence of many gods, for she speaks of 'the holy gods' (v.11). But she knew there was only one person in all the world who could interpret these words, because they came from the God whom Daniel personally knew. One person who feared the Lord was needed in these circumstances, not human experts.

Daniel is finally found. They knock on his door, and he rubs the sleep out of his eyes, and they bring him apace to meet the mightiest man in the world, whom he has loyally served for sixteen years but never spoken to. When Daniel retired that night, he little imagined that within some hours he would have to be ready to give an answer for the reason of the hope that was in him when asked by a king! The Lord Christ encouraged his disciples not to be fearful when they appeared before dignitaries, for it would be given to them in that day what they were to say. Aneurin Bevan once said that a true orator did not know what he was going to say until he had said it! So it was with Daniel. He refuses the proffered gewgaws—'give your rewards to someone else' (v.17)—he is not going to make a buck for the honour of serving the word of God. Daniel takes command of the entire situation and from the start speaks with a calm authority (vv.17-28).

God's prophet begins by reminding Belshazzar, his nobles, his wives and his concubines how God had dealt with Nebuchadnezzar. This absolute monarch had done whatever he pleased. He gave life; he took life (v.19); he dominated the world absolutely. Then in the height of his arrogance and 'hardened with pride' (v.20), God intervened and humbled Nebuchadnezzar as never a man has been humbled:

he was deposed from his royal throne and stripped of his glory. He was driven away from people and given the mind of an animal . . . until he acknowledged the Most High God is sovereign over the kingdoms of men and sets over them anyone he wishes (vv.20-21).

Daniel displays no fear as he recalls to Belshazzar this hushed-up incident of the fall of his 'father'. Then, having hammered that point home, Daniel directs his next words to Belshazzar himself: 'But you his son, O Belshazzar, have not humbled yourself, though you knew all this' (v.22). You knew, Belshazzar! Who, amongst those who knew, would ever forget when king Nebuchadnezzar 'lived with the wild donkeys and ate grass like cattle; and his body was drenched with the dew of heaven' (v.21)? 'You knew all this', Belshazzar —and so, did you humble yourself, knowing that it is a fearful thing to fall into the hands of the living God?

> Instead, you have set yourself up against the Lord of heaven. You had the goblets from his temple . . . and you and your nobles, your wives and your concubines drank wine from them. You praised the gods of silver and gold, of bronze, iron, wood and stone . . . You did not honour the God who holds in his hand your life and all your ways (vv.23-24).

That courage which Daniel had displayed as a boy was nurtured by him through the silent years for such a time as this. 'God did not give us a spirit of timidity, but a spirit of power, of love and of self-discipline', Paul tells young Timothy (2 Timothy 1:7). It was because of Belshazzar's sin of failing to humble himself and to honour God that those words written on the wall had come to the king.

Then Daniel opens up their meaning. 'This is the inscription that was written: MENE, MENE, TEKEL, PARSIN' (v.25). Three strange words. The first is *Mene* —'numbered'—'God has numbered the days of your reign' (v.26). The God who does not need to count keeps track of us. He has seen the file on our lives; he records everything about us. He has taken a comprehensive census on all mankind. Nothing has slipped by him. His omniscience shows itself in the fruits of his care for us, of which the whole human race are the beneficiaries. 'In him we live and move and have our being' (Acts 17:28). But with the good things come attendant responsibilities. People matter to their Creator—all their thoughts, their actions, their words, their sins, their good works. Did Belshazzar keep a close eye on the records that the satraps sent him from every part of the country? Did he check how the taxes were being paid? Did he keep a record of how obedient the people were? of how the judges were judging? The king did keep accounts. He counted income and expenditure. God has done the same. How is it between ourselves and God? Belshazzar, are you in the black, or are you a debtor? How important that first word is—*Mene*, 'numbered' by God. Jehovah wrote that word twice.

The second word *Tekel*, a 'shekel', is used both for a coin and a weight. Belshazzar, 'you have been weighed on the scales and found wanting' (v.27). God numbers every day of our lives, but God also weighs a life. There is nothing he does not put in his scales—DNA code with its genetic inheritance, infantile environment, family circumstances, health, IQ, talents, education, privileges, gospel opportunities, and length of days. God weighs our entire lives, and having put Belshazzar in his scales the king was found to be deficient. It was a shallow life, an empty and flimsy life for all its famous name, wealth and recorded achievements. There was nothing of the weight of God's glory at its heart. 'You have set yourself up against the Lord of heaven' (v.23). All men must appear before God to be weighed by him.

This is a moral universe, and we are made by him, in his image and for him.

The third word is *Parsin*, but when Daniel gave the interpetation he employed the singular form *peres* (v.28). The singular word means 'divided', but it sounds like the word for 'Persian', which was *paras*. There is a play on words here, linking the basic idea of division with the name of the conqueror who will divide up the nation. Belshazzar himself was to be divided. God separates. He chops up an empty life. He breaks it into pieces. He rends asunder soul and body at death. To the dust we return. All our numbered and weighed lives are also going to be divided. Men are going to be separated at death from all that they have—and Belshazzar had more than most men could dream of! Yet his worst enemies, the Medes and Persians, were going to seize it all (v.28).

The writing on the wall challenges us. Your life—does it weigh? Does your life count? Is there a battle against sin in your life? Is the fruit of the Spirit in your life? Is there prayer in your life? Is it a God-honouring life? Is it a God-pleasing life? God weighs, God scrutinises and judges your life. It is a fearful thing that we must answer to God for our lives. How can we stand before the Most Holy One?

There are four other words in a foreign language also found in the Bible. They are found on the lips of the Lord Jesus Christ as he hung on Golgotha. He cried, *'Eloi, Eloi, lama sabachthani?'* They mean, 'My God, my God, why hast thou forsaken me?' (Mark 15:34 AV). They are the answer to the question of where we can find hope if God has weighed us and found us wanting. They tell us that Christ subjected himself to the wrath of a sin-hating God. He stood in the naked flame of the awesome rectitude of the Ancient of Days, and remained there as the One made sin for us. God forsook him when he numbered his life amongst condemned sinners. He was there weighed down with the weight of our guilt. He remained hanging on the cross until his soul and body were divided from one another in death. His last act was to commend his spirit into his Father's hands, and then his body was taken down and laid in a tomb. The Word who was with God and was God became the Lamb of God. The altar on which he hung was the cross of Calvary. He was there numbered, weighed, divided and forsaken by his Father, in order that henceforth God may take us to himself, and love us with a love that will never let us go, as we go on trusting in the person and work of his Son.

In that tremendous coming day, when God will weigh the life of the church by the standards of his holy law, he never puts the church in the scales alone, but always it is the church *in Christ*. God weighs her in the Lord Jesus so that his perfect obedience to God's law becomes theirs—that weighs for them, all the weight of the good works of Jesus carries for them. A repenting sinner's life is fruitful in Christ, heavy in Christ, counting in Christ. Self-integrated and confident, he is able to say, 'I can do all things through this Christ.'

Every preacher as he preaches the gospel looks for repentance towards God and faith in the Lord Jesus Christ. Daniel had waited to see it in Nebuchadnezzar, and he looks now to see it in Belshazzar. The king was a generous man, as many people in the world are. For interpreting those words for Belshazzar, Daniel, in spite of his protestations, 'was clothed in purple, and a gold chain was placed around his neck, and he was proclaimed third highest ruler in the kingdom' (v.29).

From morning obscurity to evening exaltation! From morning anonymity to evening renown! Belshazzar was a noble king; he had made a promise (v.16) and he kept it, even though what he heard was bad news.

Some express surprise that Daniel was not thrown into prison. Where is the rage when Belshazzar heard the meaning of MENE, MENE, TEKEL, PARSIN? There was initial fear, his face turning pale, his knees knocking and his legs giving way, but at the end of the interpretation there is no angry king to be found. Belshazzar has shaken off his fright. He cannot believe the Word of God. It is the last day of his life and the last opportunity to repent, but Belshazzar is as hard as he has ever been. This half-drunken king knew those Jews. What they wanted was revenge for what he and his family had done to them. He knew of the destruction that they longed to see brought on Babylon. 'Good try, Daniel! Better luck next time!' Belshazzar recognised Daniel's abilities and he slyly winked at his lords when he heard Daniel's speech. It was a bravura performance. 'Please be upstanding. A round of applause for . . . Daniel—is that your name?' Daniel was a clever fellow in Belshazzar's eyes. and a loyal servant of the state. He had never given any trouble these many years. The king prided himself that he had an eye for talent—'The country needs a man like you. Now back to the feast. Let's pick up where we left off. Strike up the band!' They were impressed with Daniel, his presence and oratory—much better that these so-called wise men! They concluded that Daniel was a pretty clever conjurer, who was able to make hands write words on walls. 'Let's see some of our own men do the same—how about that?' So the wise man started to think what new tricks they could devise to tickle the jaded royal fancy.

But Daniel's message to the king? That left them cold. So they roundly applauded him, sang 'For he's a jolly good fellow', called for a toast in his honour, dressed him in purple and murmured about some further state recognition. But there was no 'Amen' from that company, and certainly no 'God be merciful to us sinners', because they could not comprehend Daniel. They did not know where he was coming from. They could not figure out a man for whom the greatest honours Babylon could give were evidently like a pile of dung. Daniel had no ambition to be the Chancellor of the Exchequer. He reckoned all things as loss for the excellency of knowing the Lord. Only one thing he desired, that the Word of God rule in the life of Babylon, that what had happened in Nineveh under Jonah's preaching should happen there too, that from the greatest of them to the lowest of them the court should sit down in sackcloth and ashes, crying mightily to God that he would save the nation.

What happened to Babylon? That night the river Euphrates was diverted so that it was no longer a virtual moat of defence for the city. The army of the Medes and Persians swept into Babylon. There was hardly any resistance as the people slipped away quietly, handing it over to the invaders. That night Belshazzar lay a corpse in the palace. God had said to him, 'Thou fool! This night thy soul shall be required of thee.' When men raise their glasses and say peace and safety, then sudden destruction comes upon them. The man who appointed Daniel the third in the nation was dead six hours later. That is the scene at the end of Daniel chapter 5: Belshazzar dying amidst the temple goblets from Jerusalem, the dregs of the wine still in them, upon the floor. What was his life with its drinking and feasting, its women and all its pleasures—what was that worth when it was weighed by God? 'For as the crackling of thorns under a pot, so is the laughter of the fool' (Ecclesiastes 7:6 AV). Empty, noisy, and quickly over. 'Take heed to yourselves, lest at any time your hearts be overcharged with surfeiting, and drunkenness, and cares of this life, and so that day come upon you unawares' (Luke 21:34 AV). Belshazzar died as he had lived, without God and without hope. Though he had all the wealth men dream of, the opportunity given to him by a long-suffering God at the very end of his life to confess his sin and seek the mercy of God was one he disdained. Let no one presume that they will receive the opportunity God gave the king. Behold now is the promised time, now is the day of salvation. Today, if you will hear his voice, harden not your hearts.

3
Under Darius

The triumph of effectual prayer

Darius the Mede, like hundreds of other people mentioned in the Bible, is an unknown figure from secular historical records, at least so far. Attempts have been made to identify him with different men, but without solid conviction. It seems possible that he was a leader of Median ancestry whom Cyrus 'made ruler over the Babylonian kingdom' (9:1). This period with its details of the downfall of Babylon is a little obscure: revolutions breed confusion and the pressure of instant decisions. However, we are told that during the year following the defeat of Nabonidus's army and the death of Belshazzar, while Darius was settling into power, there came a day when Daniel was studying the Bible. What he read moved him to turn in confession to God, and Daniel proceeded to pray one of the most complete and extraordinary prayers found in the Scriptures.

1. The prayer of Daniel (chapter 9)

Why is this such a perfect prayer?

1. Firstly, it is perfect because *it begins and continues in a spirit of worship.* 'O Lord, the great and awesome God, who keeps his covenant of love with all who love him

89

and obey his commands' (v.4). Daniel has been reading what the prophet Jeremiah had written, which indicated that soon the people of God would be returning home from Babylon to Jerusalem. This encouraged his praying, but he does not clamour 'Please send us home! Remember to take me home! When are we going to Jerusalem?' No, Daniel begins in adoration. God so cares for this people that he will take them back to the promised land. He will do this because he once made a covenant with their father Abraham and with Abraham's seed. This nation he loved of all the nations in the world, and his gift to them was this land. Daniel's foundation hope lay in his covenant mercy: 'O Lord, the great and awesome God who keeps his covenant of love' (v.4). Jehovah is the God you can trust, because he is absolutely straight. What he is stands in contrast to the seed of Abraham themselves. Daniel ransacks the whole vocabulary of sin in Scripture to describe this loved people's guilt: 'we have sinned and done wrong. We have been wicked and have rebelled; we have turned away from your commands and laws. We have not listened to your servants the prophets, who spoke in your name' (vv.5-6).

Those dark realities are not ignored, and guilt means that Daniel cannot start by insisting, 'Get us back home.' There are no triumphalistic assertions of big plans about rebuilding Jerusalem and the temple, because all the past generations of God's people have had a despicable history. Daniel is too wise to look at his fellow countrymen and put his confidence in their works. God alone is totally reliable. For generations these people had continued to worship golden calves and the Baals. They persecuted God's prophets and rejected his word, so that everything that subsequently happened to them they deserved. The dreadful exile and the length of their sentence in Babylon had been fair. God was perfectly right to deal with them in this way. So Daniel's prayer begins as a prayer of confession. Its hope is in a God who is light. This just God had made the perils of disobedience spectacularly clear. So Daniel cannot chant vain repetitions like the heathen, 'Two more years. Two more years. Get us home in two more years!' No way! His whole prayer is determined to justify the ways of God. In fact he does not call the Lord 'our God' until verse 9, and not until verse 17 does he ask for anything. When he does petition the Lord, it is just that God may listen: 'Now, our God, hear . . . O Lord, look with favour. . . Give ear, O God, and hear; open your eyes and see . . .' (vv.17-18). That is all he asks for—a hearing, because their sin has forfeited every right they had before God.

On one occasion the prophet Amos saw vast swarms of locusts coming like clouds to devour all the crops. He thinks of the devastation they will cause, and Amos falls in prayer before God. But what he prays for is mercy: 'Sovereign LORD, forgive! How can Jacob survive? He is so small!' (Amos 7:2). Now *we* would have focused on the locusts: 'Lord, take these locusts away.' But Amos was reflecting on the consequences of the union that the holy God has established with those who profess to be his people. There is a covenant link between sin and its consequences. 'The wages of sin is death.' Whereas this land should have been flowing with milk and honey, the locusts would 'strip the land clean' (Amos 7:2) and turn it into a wilderness. Barrenness among God's people is always caused by their rebellion. So Amos pleaded for God's forgiveness because he knew, as Daniel knew, that there were far greater dangers than the loss of crops, liberty, land, or a war. One can set out on a pattern of conduct which results in the loss of God. So Daniel begins in humble worship, as the Saviour teaches us, 'Our Father, which art in heaven, hallowed by thy name.'

2. The second reason why this is such a perfect prayer is because *there is no attempt to blame others* for the misery they are in. It is the easiest thing for a small people to blame its ills on neighbouring bigger nations; most little countries have an inferiority complex. It would have been easy for the people of God to say that the plight they were in was due to wicked Babylon. Daniel refuses to do so: 'O LORD, we and our kings, our princes and our fathers are covered with shame because we have sinned against you' (v.8). They remembered all that Babylon had done to the cities of Israel, destroying the temple and enslaving the people, but Daniel goes to the first cause of this. The Christian always goes to the first cause, which is Almighty God. That is the bedrock of Christian counselling and evangelical comfort. 'We have sinned,' he said, 'and so we have brought this inevitable divine judgment on ourselves.' God had sent prophets to them, but the people defied them and would not listen. They would not take Ezekiel or Jeremiah seriously and rather scorned them. They were later eloquent and energetic in painting the sepulchres of such prophets, saying what wonderful men they were. Inside were the bones of the prophets they had persecuted.

Neville Chamberlain once said that the responsibility for the Second World War was Hitler's alone. Great applause! Men like to hear that sort of thing: 'The problem with Europe is Germany' or 'The problem with

Europe is France.' And the problem with the church? Well, it's not us. It's modernism, or it's sacerdotalism, or it's materialism, or the bishops, or Marx, or Freud. It is always conveniently out there away from us. Daniel says that it is 'we who have sinned and done wrong. We have been wicked and have rebelled; we have turned away from your commands and laws. We have not listened to your servants the prophets' (vv.5-6). What is the difference between ourselves and the other people of our town? Are we less wicked? No, it is just that we have seen our sin for what it is. We have acknowledged our behaviour as reprehensible. We have put it before God and we have not attempted to cover it. The Lord's congregations are the only bodies in the whole world who admit and confess their sin.

I went to see a lady in hospital recently who had broken her arm. After I had talked to her I went round to the other people in their beds, and one old lady said, 'I want to die. I want to die.' I said to her, 'Well, if you die, you know, you are going to meet God, and so you must start praying now if you are soon going to meet God. This is what you must pray: "God be merciful to me a sinner."' 'I'm not a sinner', she said immediately, adding, 'And if you knew me you'd know I wasn't.' Can you imagine what psychological pressures that puts us ministers under? The hospital ward is listening on a quiet afternoon to a visiting pastor, and he meets an ill, depressed old lady, and apparently, instead of cheering her up, he is trying to point out to her that she is a lost sinner. It seems such an unkind thing for a Christian to do. But no lasting joy can come without a knowledge of our real condition before the living God. Sin, the Westminster Shorter Catechism tells us, is 'a want of conformity unto or transgression of the law of

God.' That law is summarily comprehended in the words, 'Thou shalt love the Lord thy God with all thy heart and soul. Thou shalt love thy neighbour as thyself.' Those are God's just requirements for his creatures who live in his creation. Sin is any lack of conformity at all to that. How blind the person who can say, 'I'm not a sinner'!

Daniel will not blame others, and he does not gloss over his own life. 'The Word of God came to us, and we did not listen', he is saying, and he specifies the sins that are theirs. Are you specific when you acknowledge your sin? Peter wept bitterly over a specific sin. David prayed Psalm 51 over a specific sin. The publican in the temple would not lift up his eyes and beat his bosom; it was specific sins that crushed him. There is hope even for the whole city of Sodom if there are fifty, or even twenty, who are confessing their sins. I hope in every gospel congregation there are ten men who, in solidarity with their churches, confess their sins: 'I am the unprofitable servant. I am the one who has received so many benefits and blessings, and given so little in return.'

Righteous Daniel was a forgiving man, and so could be emboldened to ask for forgiveness from a merciful God. It was John Wesley who on a voyage to America heard General Oglethorpe, the Governor of Georgia, berating a servant for drinking his entire supply of best Cyprus wine: 'This villain, Garibaldi, has drunk the lot, and he will be bound hand and foot and sent back home on a man-of-war. The rascal should have taken care how he uses me, for I never forgive.' 'Then I hope, sir, that you never sin', said Wesley, to striking effect. The Governor paused, and after a long moment threw his keys back to Garibaldi: 'There, villain, take my keys, behave better for the future.' Daniel had shown forgiveness to Nebuchadnezzar and would soon show it to Darius also. He could with good conscience seek mercy from God for his own and his people's sins.

3. It is a perfect prayer, thirdly, because *Daniel is concerned for the honour of God's name*. You see the climax of the prayer: 'Turn away your anger and your wrath from Jerusalem' (v.16), and more specifically, 'see the desolation of the city that bears your Name' (v.18), and again, 'O my God, do not delay, because your city and your people bear your Name' (v.19). Why is Daniel praying as he does? Because of what he says in those final words of the prayer: 'your city and your people bear your Name.' This is the most extraordinary name that has been revealed under heaven amongst men. Here is a God with a reputation, and these people bear his name—as if they have a T-shirt with the name of God emblazoned upon it. They willingly identify themselves with him. They tell everyone that their Redeemer has the most wonderful of names, that it is a name of transcendence, omnipotence and, especially, of grace. Yet the city that was most closely identified with that name was a heap of ruins, and the people who stood for this name were a motley crowd of prisoners of war living in rags in a ghetto in Babylon. 'We bear your name—and look at us!' they cried. Daniel was praying, 'I take your holy name on my lips when I pray to you, my Lord, but see how Babylon abuses your name with its blasphemous contempt. This world judges you when it scorns me, and your city. It sees a bunch of slaves, desolation, conquest, and the ruins of your house. What shame is being poured on your name! People think of us as a lost cause. They identify us with

defeat and decline. To them it is all over—your name is virtually that of an extinct breed of religionists. We are yesterday's men. Lord, you must act. Take the initiative. Your honour and your very reality is at stake. Your name is barely traced in the dust of the ruins of Jerusalem.'

For Daniel there was this extraordinary contrast between the glory of God's name in the past and the weakness associated with God's name now. He says, 'O Lord our God, who brought your people out of Egypt with a mighty hand and who made for yourself a name that endures to this day' (v.15). Then he looks around and in the next breath says, 'See the desolation of the city that bears your Name' (v.18). Every Christian bears God's name. They were baptised into the name of the Father, and of the Son, and of the Holy Spirit. How is it with that name today? How is it when they gather specifically in that name today? Is there power and life and love? Is it an enduring name? Is it a desolate name? And Daniel prays for the glory and honour of God revealed in his name to be seen and manifest again.

So three things make it a perfect prayer. It begins with worship. It does not make any attempt to blame others. Its passionate concern is for the honour of God's name.

There is one more thing to be said about this prayer, and it is about the occasion when it was prayed. Why did Daniel confess his sins at that moment? What made him pray? It had nothing to do with the death of Belshazzar and the trauma of that midnight hour when he was summoned out of his bed to speak so bravely and truly at that feast. The deaths he witnessed that night and the coming of a new king were not the cause of his praying. It had everything to do with the Scriptures. Daniel had been reading in his Bible the writings of the prophet Jeremiah (v. 2). When he was a young boy, Daniel's mother and father might have taken him to hear the Word of God—as many parents do. Daniel's parents were in fact actually able to bring him to hear Jeremiah preaching. The aged Daniel is now reading Jeremiah 25:12 or Jeremiah 29:10, passages in which Jeremiah tells the sinful people that they were to go into an exile that was to last seven decades. Daniel, with that same gift of prophecy that Jeremiah had, could go into the presence of God and talk to him, and could also receive a word from God which he would then bear out, burning like a fire in his bones, and declare to men. Yet Daniel, who became a vehicle of Scripture, still studies the Scriptures that holy men of God have spoken as borne along by the Spirit of God. Daniel examines the state of the church and the world about him in the light of the Bible.

How important it is to keep studying the Scriptures, and never to stop! I was staying with a pastor friend, and Larry Mills said to me, 'I've got to go and visit a lady in the congregation. She has just had a baby and her husband is a doctor in the Navy. She just came home from hospital last evening. Would you like to come with me?' So we visited their home, and there was the mother with the new-born baby. As we talked Larry asked her, 'Did you have a good night?' She smiled and said,

Not bad at all. The baby woke about half past five and I fed and changed her and then it was half past six—too late to go back to bed. So I had my quiet time. I picked up my Bible and said to the little girl as she lay in my arms, 'Now God has given us this book. This is the Word of God, and we Christians read it every day.' So I read the Bible to the child. Then I said to her, 'You know, after we've read the Word of God we pray. We speak to the Saviour who has given us this Word.' So I put her little hands together and I prayed with her.

That was her answer. Her daughter was forty-eight hours old. She was fed by her mother's milk, and then she was in that atmosphere where her soul was being fed with the milk of the Word. Before she could ever comprehend a sound, she was under the sound of those words and was the object of her mother's prayers. She opened for me a window on Christian motherhood, and on the special place that the child of a believing parent has in God's sight, a 'holy' child (1 Corinthians 7:14). It is good to remind our young people that many of them were prayed for by their mothers within minutes of being born, and that they too read the Word to them long before they could comprehend a single sound of it. Their parents could not cope with all the pressures of being parents without that Word and prayer.

As a man with the gift of prophecy Daniel had the unique privilege of speaking to God face to face, but he still studied the written Scriptures. Daniel read of an imminent ending to the captivity and a return to Jerusalem. There was nothing in the world around that suggested that within a couple of years God's people would begin the process of the long trek back to Jerusalem. Daniel's beliefs were structured by the Word of God. Noah also, two years before the flood, the vast ark almost completed, could see no signs in the cloud formations, no unusual rising of the rivers, no change in animals' behaviour, nothing at all outwardly to suggest that a great flood was soon to destroy the world. There was a divine prophecy that had come to him, maybe 120 years earlier. He believed that Word yet. Some of us have been Christians for fifty years, and we have lived for half a century obeying the commandments and believing the promises of the Bible. It has taught us how to pray and given us hope in dark days. We have cried, 'Lord, fulfil your promises.'

Why pray if God has said that he will do something? Why does the Saviour tell us to pray 'Thy kingdom come', when we know it is certainly going to come? The answer is that God has ordained the restoration of his people from Babylon through making them a different people. No longer will they be the worshippers of Baal, as they have been for centuries, but an idol-hating people, a repentant and a prayerful people. This people loves the name of the Lord above anything else in the whole world. Daniel was a spokesman for that remnant who had been purified and refined in Babylon's crucible for seventy years. His praying was evidence of the Lord's beginning to fulfil his word in Daniel's old age.

It is a *faithful* people whom the Lord restores, and Daniel is a man of faith. He believes the word in Jeremiah that God will restore them to Jerusalem. Faith is always focused upon a promise, and we should ask ourselves as we pray if we have a promise to support us—not some words that leap out of the Bible and excite us, but those 'exceeding great and precious promises' that God has given to his people through prophets and apostles. They are in the Bible through his supervision, and when Christians pray they do so with a confidence that God will fulfil them.

Being sure that there is a promise for us is crucial. God never made a promise that we would get certain grades in our exams, or that every seriously ill person would be healed, or that every poor Christian will become rich. He has promised that all things are going to work together for our good. He has promised that we can do all things through Christ who strengthens us. He has promised to teach us, in whatsoever state we are, to be content in that condition. He has promised that he will never leave us. He has promised that he is going to build his church, and the gates of hell are not going to prevail against it. Such promises are what we plead, with the certainty that they come from the throne of the universe. Luther roughly says, 'Throw God's promises right back at him!'

So Daniel was reading the Scriptures one day and he sees a promise that means that in a few years the people of God will be returning from exile. He turns that into prayer: 'For your sake, O my God, do not delay'; it has been so long, and 'your city and your people bear your Name' (v.19).

Today we are not looking forward to the restoration of Jerusalem. We are looking forward to the regeneration of all the cosmos, a new heavens and a new earth. The apostle Peter talks about that and he says, 'you look forward to the day of God and speed its coming' (2 Peter 3:12). How do we speed something whose time has been fixed and promised by Almighty God? The answer he gives is, 'You ought to live holy and godly lives' (v.11). In other words, we do so by fulfilling our calling and being true Christians in a multitude of ways: by giving an answer for the hope that is in us whenever anyone asks; by loving God with all our hearts and loving our neighbours as ourselves; by husbands loving their wives as Christ loved the church; by wives obeying their husbands; by children obeying their parents in everything; by repenting of the sins we commit. It is by being the most consistent Christians we can possibly be that we speed the day when the new heavens and earth will come. Daniel was speeding his day of restoration to Jerusalem by praying as he did.

We do not know how long Daniel prayed, but we do know that he was still praying that evening (v.21) when Gabriel came and touched him, telling him that from the first moment he had prayed heaven was listening (v.23). The angel was sent to give him that assurance, and he also spoke words to this effect: 'You've been meditating on this figure "seventy", haven't you? That number has been on your mind for days. I want to encourage you in what is going to happen in seventy periods of seven' (i.e. in 490 years' time). The messenger of God proceeded to divide up that period of almost half a millennium into three uneven parts.

1. First, there will be 'seven sevens' (v.25), about 49 years, and it will be during that period under Cyrus king of Babylon that the king will issue a decree for the Old Testament Messiahists to return and rebuild Jerusalem. This is the time of Ezra's and Nehemiah's struggles, and so it is called 'times of trouble' (v.25).

2. That will be followed by a period of 'sixty-two sevens' (v.25). That would be 434 years, and it is a mute period on the lips of Gabriel and, in fact, in the whole of the Bible. It is the period between the Old and New Testaments, when no prophets were sent by God. That silence was ultimately broken when John the Baptist began to preach.

3. Finally, there is going to be one other 'seven' (vv.26-27). During this intense period the most important events of all history will occur. Two are singled out:

i] The 'Anointed One [the Messiah] will be cut off' (v.26). He will cry, 'My God, my God, why hast thou forsaken me?' as, bearing our guilt, he is cut off from his Father's favour. He 'will have nothing' (v.26)—so total will be his rejection by men and God. Yet by this death he will put an end to Levitical 'sacrifice and offering' (v.27). A new 'covenant with many' will be confirmed in his shed blood (v.27).

ii] 'The people of the ruler who will come will destroy the city and the sanctuary' (v.26). So Jerusalem and its temple are going to be destroyed yet again. What need will there ever be for the temple, now that the Messiah has taken away the sin of the world? The ruler referred to will be the Roman prince Titus Vespasianus, and this destruction will take place in the year AD 70. 'And on a wing of the temple he will set up an abomination that causes desolation, until the end that is decreed is poured out on him' (v.27): that is, once again, as with the abominations perpetrated by Antiochus Epiphanes, heathen rites and emblems will be installed in God's temple by Titus. The destruction will continue until the decreed end. Dr Edward J. Young writes, 'The precise point of termination of the period of seventy sevens is not revealed. The emphasis, rather, is not so much upon the beginning and termination of this period as it is upon the great results which the period has been set apart to accomplish' (*The New Bible Commentary Revised*, IVP, p.700).

Daniel has lived all his life in Babylon. The return to Jerusalem during the long years of Nebuchadnezzar and Belshazzar seemed an increasingly impossible fancy. Yet the Scriptures said that in seventy years the exile would end. What lies in store for God's people? The return to Jerusalem—certainly that; but no lasting peace in this world. Hope lay not in the land but in the Lord from heaven. Let Daniel and all God's people look to him. Gabriel summarises the six Messianic accomplishments of this period of seventy sevens (v.24):

1. *Transgression will be finished.* Caused by men, sin and guilt have lived on as an ugly reality. But the Messiah will effectively put transgression away with a shout of triumph, 'It is finished!' God's alienation from us will be ended.

2. *Sin will be put to an end.* This reality of the termination of the guilt, dominion and condemnation of sin is repeated.

3. *Wickedness will be atoned for.* It will be by the sacrifice of the Messiah that the end of sin will be achieved.

4. *Everlasting righteousness will be brought in.* This righteousness was first outside this world, but it will be brought in from God through the Messiah and it replaces the sin which has been atoned for.

5. *The vision and prophecy will be sealed up and completed.* In the Old Testament dispensation the prophet represented God, who made himself known by visions to his servants. That entire prophetic institution was preparatory for the coming and words of the Son of

103

God, when the end of that anticipatory period would be sealed.

6. *The most holy will be anointed.* This phrase appears to refer to the enduing of the Messiah with the Spirit of God.

Since the promised appearing of the Messiah, the good news about him has gone out like a centrifugal force, from Jerusalem to Judea, and then to Samaria, and out to the uttermost corners of the earth. This message of his great accomplishments, finishing transgressions, putting away sin, atoning for wickedness and bringing in an everlasting righteousness, has reached the ends of the earth—even to us thousands of miles from Babylon and centuries later. It has reached the shores of the Irish Sea, and we in Wales at the end of the second millennium have come to know the benefits of his coming. We have believed in him.

2. Daniel in the den of lions (chapter 6)

When king Belshazzar had been the ruler in Babylon, he had not wanted to know of any prophet from the Lord. All that was changed when God intervened and wrote four words on the wall of the palace. Only Daniel could interpret the handwriting on the wall, and he alone of the wise men of Babylon had the authority to tell the king, 'Your kingdom is divided and given to the Medes and Persians' (5:27). Awareness of these extraordinary events made the new king, Darius the Mede, take notice of Daniel. 'It pleased Darius to appoint 120 satraps to rule throughout the kingdom, with three administrators over them, one of whom was Daniel'

(6:1). These three men would check the reports that were coming to them from the 120 satraps all over the Empire, but of these three Daniel was supreme. We are told that 'Daniel so distinguished himself among the administrators and the satraps by his exceptional qualities that the king planned to set him over the whole kingdom' (v.3). There were those amongst the 120 satraps and the two other administrators who heard of Daniel's elevation to office with deep jealousy—that a foreigner, this Old Testament Messiahist, had such power in the land! Daniel was a man of such renowned integrity, unbribable by gold, or even by a smile, and unafraid of men's frowns. He was the man who was going to monitor the bureaucracy and vested interests of Babylonia. Daniel is now in his eighties, meticulous and straight; we would say that he was 'one of the old school'.

One meets Christians like that even today. They are not always easy men to work with, because their consciences are tied to the book of God. But they are safe men as colleagues. Grudgingly admired by the world, they are sometimes treated more shamefully in evangelical congregations because they do not fit in with a casual ethos and stress upon youth leadership. In Babylon an orchestrated campaign developed to get rid of Daniel. They began by checking out on 'his conduct of government affairs' (v.4). The equivalent of the investigative journalists of Babylon were sitting at Daniel's front door, and searching through his rubbish for evidence of some misdoing. It was a forlorn task. They found no dirty linen at all. Daniel lives a modest, self-denying, sleaze-free life. He is a man of total honesty with nothing to hide. They had to give their own rueful testimony to his integrity: 'They could find no corruption in him, because he was trustworthy, and neither corrupt nor negligent' (v.4).

Although no sins of Daniel are recorded in Scripture, we know that Daniel was not a sinless man because in his prayer he stands with the people and acknowledges his own shortcomings. Daniel was a man of like passions as ourselves, but each day on at least three occasions he got down on his knees and appropriated his Saviour. God was his refuge and strength. Daniel was about eighty-five, but undiminished. He was not a nostalgic man looking back to 'good old days'. Daniel would say, 'I live by faith in God. He makes me more than conqueror.' That is where he got this exceptional endurance, so that in old age he was abounding in God's work. When he was set over the whole kingdom he didn't wink at the world and think that all is fair in politics. He didn't say to himself, 'I'll cheat as little as I can. I'll turn a blind eye to things just very infrequently.' He didn't plead, 'Well, a man has to live.' Daniel hated the smallest sin and was 'neither corrupt nor negligent' (v.4). To sustain himself on that narrow path he went to the secret place three times each day.

When the gates of hell want to destroy Daniel, that secret place is where they attack him. They will use his piety against him. They will point at his praying and his seriousness about divine things. They know there is no hope of attacking him anywhere else. If they make false accusations that Daniel is putting his hand in the till, no one will believe them. One thing they can guarantee about Daniel is that he will not stop praying. So the administrators and satraps go as a group to Darius the mighty conqueror, and they persuade him to issue a decree forbidding prayer for a month except to himself. Darius is easy to persuade. He would be a god for thirty

106

days. Why not? He could see the advantages of that. There would be no more differences of religion in the Empire. Names and sects and parties would fall. 'Darius the god' would be all in all. He would be the one deity worshipped in all the empire. What a unifying factor in this cosmopolitan state! Perhaps after the thirty-day trial period the people would like it so much that they would want to keep it.

What about Daniel? The delegation who had spoken to the king knew it was impossible for him to go without praying for a month. Actually for him not to pray for a day would have been an impossibility, so they thought they had snared Daniel. This book of Daniel is a history of a great battle that is continually taking place between the kingdoms of this world and the kingdom of God, between Satan and Christ. When the satraps want to remove Daniel from office, they choose to do it by discrediting him, and self-promotion is their only purpose. Satan has another scheme: he wants to stop Daniel praying. Satan doesn't care if he continues as the Prime Minister; his concern is Daniel's intercession.

Imagine if I opened a curtain on one side to reveal a lion ready to pounce, but when I opened the other end of the curtain there was Satan prepared to devour us. Whom would you fear more? You say that you would be more afraid of Satan. But there are evidently Christians who are more afraid of lions than they are of Satan. As well as the lions at the end of this chapter, there is a lion at its beginning. Satan is like a roaring lion, and as he goes about looking for anyone he can devour, this man is a prime target. He wants to stop Daniel addressing the throne of grace. In other words, there is an easy way to dodge the threat of lions' dens, and that is to stop praying. Dangers which we cannot see with our eyes or hear with our ears are far more threatening than visible things. It was wonderful when Daniel braved the lions' den. It was more wonderful when he constantly overcame his laziness, his cold heart, the temptations of the flesh, and turned away from a hundred and one other details claiming his attention. Daniel bowed before God and prayed day after day, with principalities and powers and rulers of the darkness of this world working all around him to stop him seeking the face of God. The great miracle in Daniel 6 is that he continued to pray.

If the people of God stop praying, then no lions will threaten them. The boss will stop grumbling at you. Your unconverted family will think you are 'normal' again. Life would be far easier at that level if Christians stopped praying, because the lions win when we are silent. The great mark of true faith is that we keep praying. It shows that we fear God more than we fear men. Satan could see what being at the throne of grace had done for Daniel for over eighty years. There were lessons he had learned at the feet of the Lord that he could not have learned anywhere else. Satan knew that the church would triumph in Babylon only if it went in its weakness to God and asked for grace. That would be a church with a future, for God is not deaf to such a people. When it is pitch black, all you need is a single light and then darkness no longer prevails. The destiny of the church in Babylon was decided in Daniel's room. The great battle took place there—not in the lions' den, but at the open window looking to God. What were the snarls of lions compared to that warfare?

We are told that Daniel prayed three times a day (v.10): that is, Daniel prayed more than a thousand times every year. If each of us prayed as often as Daniel prayed, then by the time of the next Conference this congregation would have prayed more than a million times! That will not be easy. Prayer is inconvenient, because there is always something else to do, and many sins hinder us. In real prayer there are routine clichés that have to be killed, pious mumbles and rhythms to break down. Yet prayer is as essential as the breathing of the soul, and without it our soul dies. In prayer we articulate our faith and live it out. If a law were passed in Wales that prohibited anyone praying during the next month, most Welshmen could very self-righteously keep that law with little or no inconvenience, except for a feeling of outrage at the loss of civil liberties. It would make no difference to the lives of most people. But what is frightening is how many Christians live without prayer; how many church officers, ministers and preachers live without prayer. Why don't we make an impact on the nation? Why isn't the church stronger? Why aren't there more conversions? Because the plot against Welsh pray-ers has succeeded! Yet, why are we as strong as we are? Why are we as full of grace as we are? Why are there conversions? Because the plot against Welsh pray-ers has failed. There are men and women of prayer in the land.

But there is something more wonderful. There is somebody exalted to the right hand of God, and he ever lives to make intercession for us. Sometimes we are so moved by someone's praying for us at a crisis in our lives. Their prayers have lifted us, and we go in the strength of that intercession for a few days. Then we think to ourselves, 'Here am I so encouraged by my friend or my pastor praying for me like that, but at God's right hand I have someone constantly whispering my worthless name in the ears of his Father in heaven, and so he saves me to the uttermost. Christ takes my prayers and de-sins them, making them a sweet savour to God.' Our prayer today should be not 'Make me like Daniel' but 'Make me like the Lord Jesus.'

When the state tells you to do something that God forbids, then, with all the reluctance in the world, you have to disobey Caesar. So when Daniel knew that the decree was signed, immediately he went home and prayed. He behaved as he always did, no matter how many laws of the Medes and Persians were forbidding his conduct. If God's Word for you is more than a great old book or a useful standard of conduct, then Daniel's response will find an echo in you. There have been times when you have read it and have clutched that Bible to you with a lump in your throat thinking, 'How wonderful! I have the word of God! I have this book that comes from another world!' The prayer that then follows will not be a tedious formality; it will be a river of life, a consuming fire which nothing can extinguish. How can you ban such prayer? It is laughable. It is like forbidding the tides, or prohibiting lightning. You stop praying, and you sign your death warrant. Only someone who has never prayed will not pray for a month. Daniel could not stop praying if there were as many lions in Darius's den as there are slates on the roofs of Aberystwyth!

It is as impossible to stop praying as it is for the Christian to cease to be grateful for his salvation. So Daniel couldn't stop being Daniel, and he knew exactly what he was doing when he went to his room to pray. The text makes that transparently clear. When Daniel learned that the decree had been published he went to his room. Daniel did not fall into some trap. Daniel did not intend to plead, 'I didn't know.' He knew the decree, and the consequences of defiance. He went to that upper room and laid his life on the line, as if he were deliberately walking to the gallows. He went 'just as he had done before' (v.10). That day was no different. It was just an ordinary time of prayer. There is no need to embellish that. Nothing is said in the Bible about what Daniel felt; we are simply told what he did.

If anyone had stopped Daniel and asked him, 'Do you feel torn between the choices of serving the king and serving God?' Daniel would have replied that there was only one option. Have you come across Christians who are always meeting problems of guidance in the Christian life? They have 'problems' about courtship, or about worship, or about recreation, or about fellowship, or about Sundays. Poor Christians, it is so perplexing for them to follow the Lord. But many so-called problems relate at root to the cost of obedience rather than inadequate guidance. It is not that they do not know what to do, but rather that the narrow path is a lonely one for this next stretch, or the cross the Saviour has given them to carry is particularly heavy. What faced Daniel was not a matter of guidance but of fundamental obedience in his life. Who was Daniel's Lord?

So Daniel 'got down on his knees and prayed'. What was the theme of his praying?—'giving thanks to his God' (v.10). He was so grateful that God knew him and that he knew the Lord. Such faith is the victory that overcomes the world. When we know God, we also know who we ourselves are, and we know our duty. We don't just scratch our noses in a restaurant before we eat; we pray. No one has to close his eyes to pray. There are times when a sick old lady in a hospital says, 'If you knew me, you'd know I wasn't a sinner', and all

111

the ward seems to be listening for your answer. No one needs to close his eyes when he prays for help on such occasions. Daniel could have continued for a whole month to pray inwardly. He needn't have gone to his room to pray, need he? He needn't have kneeled down before the windows opened towards Jerusalem. 'Avoid needless offence', people are telling us all the time. We are told that if we were not so American, or so Welsh, or so uneducated, or so cerebral, or so traditionalist, or so old, or so young, or so theological, or so untheological, we would behave in a different way. 'Those evangelicals,' people mutter, 'they've got difficult personalities, haven't they?' So men array before us the alleged benefits of belonging to the coming hyper-denomination ('It's just around the corner'), and of the healing nature of inter-faith meetings in a divided society. What we believe, we are told, is 'just your opinion'. Certainly no one has the right to be a bigot, or an ignoramus, or an obscurantist, or to hate his neighbour. Rather let us, like the Lord Jesus, grow in favour with men, be loving neighbours, and do good to all men. Above all, let us do what God says and believe what God has revealed.

If Daniel had acted according to the advice of worldly-wise men, his life of usefulness would have been all over—eating the royal food and drinking the royal wine as a teenager. But God had had the prior claim to Daniel's life for more than threescore years and ten. If we looked through the windows of Daniel's home we would be seeing the greatest statesman of his age, maybe of any age, and he is on his knees speaking to God, just like that mother we mentioned. She was nursing a 48-hour-old baby and speaking to the same heavenly Father that Daniel was addressing. This colossus was praying simply like a child in his Father's presence.

What greater hope could there be for the future of our nation than to have statesmen like that?

I was visiting a Presbyterian minister in Inverness. He had once been a pastor in Canada, and when the former Lord Chancellor had cause to visit Toronto he would ask if he might stay with him and enjoy Highland fellowship. Once when he was staying at the manse the pastor said to the statesman that it was a mission week and they were visiting some homes. The statesman volunteered to go with them, and so they entered a run-down tenement block full of the alienated and dispossessed members of society. They knocked on one door, and there stood a single mother who invited them in. The minister told me how he sat quietly and listened to the statesman as he went through the gospel point by point with this young girl, who had no idea that she was listening to a man who held one of the greatest offices in the British nation. Can you think of more hope for the next millennium than for a nation to have leaders like that?

After Daniel had given thanks we are told that he was 'asking God for help' (v.11). Both he and all the people of God with whom he stood in the solidarity of faith needed divine assistance. We are told that as a stranger amongst the Babylonians he opened the windows of his home towards Jerusalem, to God's 'beautiful land' which was then like a wilderness. Are we above the use of such a lawful stimulus to prayer as that? Are there not remembrances of God's mighty works in our land that can stir us to pray at this hour? If Daniel, so methodical and regular in prayer, appreciated his windows being open to Jerusalem, we must see whether our sloth needs such stimulants. When we feel ourselves to be too sluggish in prayer, we may collect all the aids which can arouse our feelings and warm our hearts.

Daniel also 'got down on his knees and prayed' (v.10). The Lord Jesus Christ spoke of the Pharisees who prayed on tiptoe so that everybody could see what they were doing (Matthew 6:5). We are told that the Lord Jesus knelt to pray (Luke 22:41). If anyone had the right to be casual and folksy with God, chatting away with the Ancient of Days, it would have been he who was in the beginning with God and in the beginning was God. But when as the God-man he spoke to his Father from this fallen world he knelt down. There was no sin in him, and nothing to bring a frown to the countenance of his heavenly God, but as a creature, a real human being, he got on his knees. That posture of Jesus tells us a lot about acceptable worship. Let us, like Daniel, 'be thankful, and so worship God acceptably with reverence and awe, for our God is a consuming fire' (Hebrews 12:28).

Then the officials of Babylon went out hunting! These elite men, the cream of Babylonian society, with all their education and everything that Babylon could offer them, 'went as a group' (v.11). Imagine it! Someone notices this band of self-important officials purposefully hurrying along the road. 'Where are you going—for a meal? ' 'No.' 'Going to the Baths?' 'No.' 'Going to see the Hanging Gardens?' 'No.' 'Going hunting?' 'No.' (It was getting embarrassing.) 'Fishing?' 'No. If you must know, we are going to catch a man praying.' These are diplomats, the Foreign Office of Babylon, and they are out hunting an old man whom they think they have caught in their trap. They intend to find him on his knees worshipping God.

Having caught Daniel in prayer, the men reported

back to Darius, telling him that they had caught a revolutionary red-handed. 'Well done, men', said the king. 'Bring in the traitor!' they cry, and in comes old Daniel. When Darius heard what had happened he was deeply humbled. We are told, 'he was greatly distressed' (v.14). What a fool he had been! He was sorry for Daniel, and for Babylon. He was sorry for these idiots because of the malice that festered in their hearts. Sorry, sorry, sorry! Don't we know such times? All day he tormented himself—was there a way out? He was 'determined to rescue Daniel and made every effort until sundown to save him' (v.14). But Darius is trapped in the snare he has himself created. The king had lost his freedom in Babylon because his pride had enslaved him. Freedom is a state of mind. Daniel was as free as a bird in Babylon. Peter in prison could sleep so soundly that an angel coming into the room couldn't wake him. 'He struck Peter on his side and woke him up. "Quick, get up!" he said' (Acts 12:7). Daniel knew God could close the mouth of every lion if he were pleased to spare his servant. All Darius had were the clichés of religion, but none of its reality: 'May your God, whom you serve continually, rescue you!'(v.16). Darius is like any number of politicians or comedians who end their routine with a weak 'God bless'.

So into the den of lions went Daniel. The den would be in cellars, with an opening for food which would have to be officially sealed, it being too easy otherwise for people, having killed someone, to dispose of his body by night through that dark opening. The king would have a signet ring and the nobles would have their signet rings, and they officially sealed the end of Daniel. But the victory was not won when he was thrown into the den of lions, nor even when he was drawn out of it. It was won in Daniel's room when he prayed.

That night another king of Babylon could not sleep (cf. 2:1), nor could he eat (v.18), because of the activity of the living God. At first light, as the weak sun was shining over Babylon, 'the king got up and hurried to the lions' den' (v.19). There he shouted for Daniel with a voice of anguish, 'Daniel, servant of the living God, has your God, whom you serve continually, been able to rescue you from the lions?' (v.20). Daniel responds from that dark, stinking hole graciously and correctly: 'O king, live for ever! My God sent his angel, and he shut the mouths of the lions' (v.21). Where do you find true majesty? It is not always found in a palace in the behaviour of members of a royal family. But it can be found in a stinking den of animals. Composure, dignity and peace there, while fear and worry rage in a king!

How was Daniel saved? Two answers are given to us. The first is from Daniel's perspective, and it is spelled out in Hebrews 11—it was by faith that Daniel 'shut the mouths of lions' (v.33). That truth is also found in our narrative: 'when Daniel was lifted from the den, no wound was found on him, because he had trusted in his God' (v.23). Daniel's confidence was in God, believing that if the Lord had willed it, then not one lion would harm him. He believed that God had the supreme authority to change the instincts of wild beasts and make them like playful kittens. So, with that calm assurance, into the den he went. Daniel knew that he was not going alone; there was a sovereign Protector with him. Faith in God keeps each Christian safe.

The second reason that Daniel was saved was that during that evening, when all the angels of heaven gathered together to receive their night duties from

116

their Lord, one of them was given this extraordinary task: 'Go to Babylon. There my beloved servant Daniel is to be thrown into a den of lions. Keep the mouth of every lion closed.' That angel came at the speed of divinity and did God's bidding (v.22).

Of course, those two reasons are inseparable. Believing prayer pulls down divine aid. When Peter is in prison, the church is praying and the angel delivers him. The excitement of this chapter is not the deliverance, but the trust. God does not always rescue his faithful servants from the stake. Daniel's miraculous deliverance is exceptional. The question is always decided by the issue of what gives greater glory to God. Oftentimes martyrdom does that. But in this instance God determined that Daniel was of more use to him alive. He has a work for Daniel yet to do, and grace to perform it. Richard Baxter wrote,

> Lord, it belongs not to my care
>   Whether I die or live;
> To love and serve Thee is my share,
>   And this Thy grace must give.

There was to be yet another monarch over Babylon, named Cyrus. God had prophesied (Isaiah 45:1) that a king bearing that name would be the one to restore his people. Daniel will be given grace to serve God and his cause under Cyrus. So the prophet is delivered from death, and Darius is more confirmed than ever in the indispensability of Daniel. He issues a decree to his entire empire that all must fear and reverence the God of Daniel. He extols the power of Daniel's Lord in the most God-honouring language, adding ultimately, 'He has rescued Daniel from the power of the lions' (vv.26-

117

27). So, far from being cruelly murdered, 'Daniel prospered during the reign of Darius and the reign of Cyrus the Persian' (v.28).

As we turn away from this great historical event, let us think of another man, greater than Daniel, let down into a pit of death, and a great stone rolled across its entrance and sealed. Do you remember that when the angels were gathered before God to receive instructions for that day, one was sent (Was it the same angel? One day we will know!) to roll the stone away. From that den of death came forth the Prince of life. He is the one who has conquered death and has kept it dead for ever and ever. So that today, to be absent from the body is not to be dead, but to be present with the Lord.

He is Daniel's God.
He is Jehovah Jesus.
He is our Saviour!

4
Under Cyrus
The return and the future

The period described in the last section of the book of Daniel begins 'in the third year of Cyrus king of Persia' (10:1), that is, 537 BC. And where was Daniel? Why should that question be asked? Because in the first year of Cyrus the Jews were given permission to return to Jerusalem, and the trickle home, which lasted a century or more, began. They had been in Babylon since being taken there as prisoners in 605 BC, and for many of them the hope of returning to their own land had not vanished. Despite all the pressure, they had not become absorbed into Babylonian culture and religion. We read in the book of Nehemiah (who lived almost a hundred years after Daniel) of 42,000 Messiahists who had made the long walk home to Israel. So, in the third year of Cyrus, where was Daniel? After bidding farewell to many fellow believers the old man was still there in Babylon, in the Persian court. We know he was not indifferent to the land of his fathers; his shutters were open to Jerusalem as he prayed. Yet he remains in exile.

Presumably we would not have ended this book with Daniel in Babylon. If this had been some work of dramatic fiction, then our ending would have been for Daniel to return as the grand old man of a newly built Jerusalem, taking the chief part in the dedication services of the temple. In fact, the book of Daniel ends with the words 'allotted inheritance', which promise

119

something far more permanent and glorious than a piece of real estate at the eastern end of the Mediterranean!

Why did Daniel stay on in Babylon? We may only conclude that he knew this to be God's will. There was yet more work for this old man to perform in his exile. All Christians have plans and dreams for the future, but most of all we want God's will for the few years that lie ahead; and being certain that something is God's will for us will save us from becoming bitter or plaintive. 'Thy will be done'—a commitment to that principle is the secret of the rare jewel of Christian contentment.

Cyrus's heart was in the Lord's hands, and he had made the king favourably disposed to the people of God, though they were facing many enemies, openly and secretly. Their foes were stirring up trouble in the Persian court, making false allegations about the Jews to Cyrus so that the city and the temple in Jerusalem might never be rebuilt. Daniel was kept in that court by God, with all the added authority that the prophet's age, office and integrity could command. Daniel is there before the king to plead the cause of the people of God as they return to Jerusalem. He is also in Babylon, more importantly, to plead knowledgeably before the courts of heaven for his people. Daniel did as much for Israel by staying in Babylon as the men with swords and trowels were doing in rebuilding the walls of Jerusalem.

1. Daniel's vision of a man (chapter 10)

During that third year of Cyrus a revelation was given to Daniel (v.1), and its theme was one of great conflict to come. It so overwhelmed Daniel that he mourned for three weeks. He is now in his late eighties, approaching the end of his life, and the message that came to him of the future was not that he would enjoy an Indian summer and a new dawn of peace, but the very reverse. The divine revelation spoke precisely of 'a great war' (v.1). In May 1970 Dr Martyn Lloyd-Jones was preaching at the graduation services of students who had completed their years at the Westminster Theological Seminary in Philadelphia. He preached to them a message from 1 Corinthians 15 on 'Holding on to the Fundamentals of the Faith', urging them always to contend for truth. The fundamentals mentioned in that chapter are that Christ died for our sins, and that he was raised on the third day according to the Scriptures. In a poignant moment in that message he spoke of the necessity laid on him to go on and on fighting for the gospel and never to stop. He alluded to Matthew Arnold's poem *Sohrab and Rustum* as mirroring his own experience, quoting these words:

> And now in blood and battles was my youth,
> And full of blood and battles is my age,
> And I shall never end this life of blood.

Daniel as a youth entered into conflict for the Messiah, and now as an old man he is still battling on. That is the Christian pattern, the consequence of serving God in a world that is at enmity against him. Our pilgrimage goes from the hard to the difficult, and from the difficult to the impossible. It is a very sad Christian life if that is not the way it is with you. 'If thou hast run with the footmen, and they have wearied thee, then how canst thou contend with horses? and if in the land of peace, wherein thou trustedst, they wearied thee, then how wilt thou do in the swelling of Jordan?' (Jeremiah 12:5 AV).

In this divine revelation of 'a great war', the old man Daniel saw a bloodstained future stretching out for the people of God in the years to come. It is as if someone in Wales back in 1907, ninety years ago, could have seen a revelation of what would characterise the world during the twentieth century. One can imagine that Welshman, too, mourning and fasting for three weeks (vv.2-3). But we are also told what Daniel did in addition to that: he set his mind to gain understanding and to humble himself before his God (v.12). He refused to panic; he used his intelligence and thought about things; he sought to gain understanding. When a man becomes a Christian he begins to use his mind as he has never used it before. Daniel would know that the Lord has never promised us anything less than trials. The table he spreads for us is in the presence of our enemies (Psalm 23). Did Christ not speak of tribulation? Were we not told that if any man followed the Lord Jesus he must bear his cross? Did the Messiah not say words to the effect that if the world hated him, then the more like him his followers lived, the more they would be hated too?

Daniel does not cry out, 'Not fair! No, Lord!' He humbles himself before God, and he is in a heavy spirit of mourning for three weeks. When God spoke to him, he told Daniel that his prayer had been heard since the first day that he prayed (v.12). The beginnings of his stumbling response to that awesome revelation were registered in heaven. Daniel had no assurance of that, but he went on praying in faith for three more weeks. 'Give me understanding', he had cried; but nothing came. He prayed on, knocking at heaven's door. He mourned and fasted, we are told (vv.2-3). Then, after three long weeks, Daniel went on with the administration of the Babylonian state. The long session of prayer came to an end, and he returned to his sphere of duty.

On 24 January 537 BC (v.4), when Daniel was with a group of men visiting a place on the bank of the river Tigris, he looked up—and there standing before him was the most breathtaking sight he had ever seen. It was a sight far more glorious than anything Babylon had ever erected. Everything that could be made by the most skilful craftsmen of Nebuchadnezzar, Belshazzar, Darius and Cyrus (all put together) paled into insignificance beside this figure. It was the same glorious person that Ezekiel had seen in the opening chapter of his prophecy; that Isaiah saw in the temple high and lifted up (Isaiah 6); that the three disciples saw on the Mount of Transfiguration; that Saul of Tarsus saw on the Damascus Road, and that John saw on the Isle of Patmos. Daniel saw him too. The men who were with him were not granted this sight; they were overwhelmed with the awe of the place and 'fled and hid themselves' (v.7). It was the Messiahist who was given the revelation. What Daniel saw was 'a man dressed in linen, with a belt of the finest gold around his waist. His body was like chrysolite, his face like lightning, his eyes like flaming torches, his arms and legs like the gleam of burnished bronze, and his voice like the sound of a multitude' (vv.5-6). The sight and the presence of this man overwhelmed Daniel, just as it overwhelmed Peter in the boat, Saul on the road, and John on the island. Daniel tells us, 'I had no strength left, my face turned deathly pale and I was helpless . . . I fell into a deep sleep, my face to the ground' (vv.8-9).

A man was once hanging about waiting to tell John

123

MacArthur something. When the opportunity came he shared with John MacArthur how he often saw the Lord, that he had visions of him and Jesus talked with him often. 'For example,' he said, 'he'll come and speak to me while I am shaving.' John MacArthur responded, 'I have just one question. Do you stop shaving?' When God appeared to the prophets and the apostles it was utterly devastating. They collapsed before him like a tree being felled. On their faces they fell, not backwards, and none of them laughed. It was a revelation of the glory of God, and it was always accompanied by a message. The vision never came mute.

God tells Daniel, 'your words were heard, and I have come in response to them' (v.12). Those words had been spoken over three weeks earlier, and Daniel had had to wait all that time to know that God was listening. What might have happened in three weeks? Might everything have been lost? Yet his prayer had reached God's ears immediately. Our prayers too are heard just as quickly as Daniel's. It is not that if we go on praying for long enough, then eventually God may hear us. From the very moment when we set our minds to gain understanding and to humble ourselves before our God, our words are heard. 'Since the first day'—that is quick, but God can reply even faster than that! He sometimes answers us *before* we call on him. Why did one week go by, then two, and then three entire weeks—and Daniel still had no light, no assurance that God had heard his prayer? The answer is very simple. God often makes his people wait a while before they see the answer. It could be twenty-one days before the answer comes, or maybe twenty-one years; and sometimes we never see the answer with our own eyes.

In the 1650s John Flavel was preaching one Sunday

in his church in Dartmouth in Devon, and a 15-year-old boy named Luke Short was in the congregation. At the end of his sermon John Flavel prayed, asking God's blessing on that message. Soon afterwards that teenager set sail from Dartmouth and emigrated to New England, in North America. When Luke Short was a hundred years old, all the horrors of dying without Christ were impressed upon him. He remembered the effects of the truths that Flavel had preached to him eighty-five years earlier—he had never been able to shake them off —and he was converted. (The incident is reported in *The Mystery of Providence* by John Flavel, Banner of Truth, p.11.) John Flavel did not know that that prayer of his was going to be answered so many decades later, but seeing things is not important: 'blessed are those who have not seen and yet have believed' (John 20:29). Even if we had seen no answers to prayer (and I cannot believe that to be the case in a company of people like this), we yet believe that God hears immediately when we pray. Without delay the Lord is weighing, judging, knowing everything and assessing what is best for us and most to his glory.

The glorious man who speaks to Daniel confirms the inevitability of the 'great war' that had been revealed to him. He speaks first of the reality of spiritual conflict, before turning (in chapter 11) to nations at war. He tells Daniel that he has been resisting Satan's work in Persia these past twenty-one days (v.13). Of course, he has been doing a billion other things, but this area which was on Daniel's heart has not been neglected. He wants to assure him that the people of God in Babylon are being shepherded. They have been under attack, but omnipotent grace has been building his church and saving his people. Daniel must know that the Lord of glory is protecting the church in Persia as it battles with principalities, powers and the rulers of the darkness of this world, just as he is helping the Messiahists in Greece (v.20).

The devil is not omniscient. But though he does not know everything he is highly organised; he has an intricate network. Nothing is haphazard, and attention is given even to the smallest detail. Demons are not like dogs let loose in a park, chasing butterflies, sniffing at this bit of grass and at that tree trunk. They plan; they are structured. The devil's assistants are more cunning than diplomats, and their servants more beautiful than angels of light. The devil has a fifth column, and it operates in every area all over the world. He stirs up prejudice against the church of Christ, always seeking to resist the spread of the gospel and the building of God's kingdom.

What of so-called 'territorial spirits'? The claim is made that these references to 'the prince of the Persian kingdom' (v.13) and 'the prince of Greece' (v.20) require us to believe that every community has 'territorial spirits' who rule over them and blind the inhabitants to the truth of the gospel. The claim is further made that there exist super-Christians with esoteric knowledge who know the actual names and jurisdictions of these spirits. They are able to bind those 'princes', release the captives and enable multitudes to come to faith in Christ. Chuck Lowe lectures at the Singapore Bible College and is the author of a helpful book, *Territorial Spirits and World Evangelism* (OMF/Mentor). He points out that there is no indication in the Bible that Satan uses a special class of geographically specific demons to hold unbelievers in darkness; nor is there any biblical evidence that Satanic opposition can be overcome by the simple expedient of naming and binding demons. The prince of Persia and the prince of Greece were not two demons whose defined tasks were to guard those two areas in perpetuity. No one can possibly affirm that there are 'guardian demons'. Persia itself waxed and waned as a power; its boundaries shrank; it became absorbed by other nations and cultures. So it has been with Greece. The book of Revelation describes Pergamum as the throne and dwelling of Satan (2:13), Smyrna and Philadelphia as locations of synagogues of Satan (2:9; 3:9), and Thyatira as the place where the teachings of Satan had entered the church (2:24). Such references are to the hostile Jews of Smyrna and Philadelphia, who were constantly stirring up the persecution of servants of the Lord Jesus so that their synagogues were carrying out the activities of God's supreme adversary. Pergamum was the official cult centre of the worship of the Roman emperor in Asia, and so had become the heart of Satan's activity in this religion in the East—as Rome was in the West. When any political powers, religious organisations, false teachings or even personal agendas obstruct the work of God, they become for that period instruments or princes of Satan. This is what the reference to the 'prince of Persia' in Daniel 10 is teaching.

How can Satan be defeated? The glorious one seen by Daniel has successfully resisted him, and he is the one who was to come in the flesh and decisively defeat the powers of darkness by his life and death. The rule of Satan over the Gentiles has ended. The Lord Christ deposed him at the cross (John 12:31; 16:11; Revelation 12:7-9). The gospel now goes outside the boundaries of Israel into every nation in the world. But, as a wounded and cornered animal, Satan will never stop attacking the people of God. To defeat him, they must do what Daniel did: humble themselves, fast, pray and go about their duties faithfully, growing in influence as they serve God with a pure conscience. 'Resist the devil, and he will flee from you' (James 4:7). Daniel sees 'a great war' ahead, but a pledge of the victory is given him: the Lord Sabaoth's Son is resisting Satan's devices in Babylon where the fight is the hottest. The devil is seeking to turn the court against the people of God returning to Jerusalem. His ultimate intention is to prevent the Messiah being born one day in that land, amongst his own and according to promise.

We are not ignorant of Satan's devices, because we have our Bibles. The Lord Jesus once said to Simon Peter, 'Satan has asked to sift you as wheat. But I have prayed for you' (Luke 22:31). That is what we see here. Satan is sifting the people of God who are under Persian and Greek influence, but the great Captain of our salvation is building his church there. When the first wave of Jews returned to Israel and began rebuilding Jerusalem, there were minor diplomats filled with hatred at this development. Men called Rehum and Shimshai became virtual princes of Satan in their activities as they opposed the establishing of the kingdom of God. Wherever there is a flock of Christ's sheep, there are wolves that want to destroy them. Whenever the church advances, dark principalities are at work. There is a great Reformation, and soon the backlash of a counter-Reformation appears. There is the Puritan period, and it is not long before Unitarianism emerges. There is the rise of heart religion, and then cerebral intellectualism appears. There is a fervent religious awakening, with spontaneous preaching that touches the masses, and then there comes an insistence on a learned ministry. Dark influences can promote fashions. One way of life becomes the new goal for the church. For example, in the first century, all things Greek became enviable: its way of life, philosophy, poetry, architecture, laws, writings, and wisdom. 'The Greeks seek after wisdom', observed the apostle Paul (1 Corinthians 1:22). A 'prince of Greece' was selling that effectively to the world.

The writings of Abraham Kuyper of Holland contain many references to the 'spirit of the time'. He once pointed to the unusual fact that we can find a certain heresy knocking at the door of the church in several places at the same time, yet without apparent collusion. One thinks of how the legalisation of abortion in the 1960s spread from country to country within a few years. There are various aspects and factors which explain the 'spirit of the age'—public opinion, the style and fashion of life, and the general way of thinking and speaking; but those factors are not in themselves sufficient explanation for what is happening. There is also a 'common moving power', which escapes our analysis and is caused by mysterious influences from the myriad principalities of the world of darkness.

The power of the Captain of our salvation is needed to resist such a spirit, that we may stand in an evil day, and having done all, to stand. 'Do you know why I've come to you?' asks Jehovah Jesus. 'Soon I will return to fight against the prince of Persia, and when I go the prince of Greece will come' (v.20). He is warning Daniel of new perils, and that he must be on his guard. Christians absolutise an enemy. They focus their powers on resisting one cult or one heresy. But the beast that comes from the sea has seven heads, not one. If you succeed in cutting off one, there are still others to attack you. Daniel must not think victory over Persia will bring Utopia. The prince of Greece is coming, and after him new threats.

'Daniel, you must watch and pray, for a principality is coming.' Old Daniel was much wiser than young Peter. Old Daniel did not say, 'That's all right, Lord. If all the others run away in panic, you just count on me.' Daniel knew his own heart better than Peter did. He had also experienced something of Satan's attacks across his long life. We are told that Daniel took the vision containing this warning with deep seriousness. He bowed with his face toward the ground; he was speechless. When someone helped him to speak, all he could say was: 'I am overcome with anguish because of the vision, my lord, and I am helpless. How can I, your servant, talk with you, my lord? My strength is gone and I can hardly breathe' (vv.16-17).

This is a man who through all his life has been brave. What courage he had showed when confronting Nebuchadnezzar as a teenager and, years later, Belshazzar when awakened from his sleep, and, later still, when thrown into a den of lions by Darius's men! But here he stands where we all one day must stand—before him who is without beginning, without ending; a God who is infinite, eternal, unchangeable in his being, wisdom, power, holiness, justice, goodness and truth; the one before whom we float like infinitely small specks on his eternal vision. How insignificant we are before him! In addition, this Lord is telling Daniel of Satan's war with the church, and Daniel needs to be strengthened to receive the message (v.19). Many Christians know such experiences, when personal attacks of the evil one have been rending times, when a consciousness of his malice has torn them apart. We have known what it is to be steadily engulfed with multiple waves of anger, bitterness, self-pity, malice and frustration. We have experienced this when driving across the Welsh hills, and have had to stop the car and get out. We are acquainted with such devices. Satan wants to destroy the peace and assurance of every one of us. Daniel's strength vanishes at the nearness of the Holy One of Israel and the knowledge of the great war, and it is then that this act of divine pity comes: 'the one who looked like a man touched me and gave me strength. "Do not be afraid, O man highly esteemed," he said' (v.19). The one who looked like a man is saying, 'I really love you.' Then he adds, 'Peace! Be strong now; be strong.' Daniel who trembled at the Word of God was strengthened by it. Everything that permanently transforms and elevates men comes to them via the Word.

There is nothing like the Bible, is there? We have gone to church thinking we believe nothing. We've climbed those pulpit steps and thought, 'If they only knew what a hypocrite was standing in front of them!' We have started to worship God. We have sung ourselves into faith. We have read ourselves into hope. We have prayed ourselves into trust. We have preached ourselves into assurance. Not in hours, but in minutes. The congregation has been awakened too. The Word has done it. 'When he spoke to me, I was strengthened', testifies Daniel (v.19). The prophet could face the future saying, 'Speak, my lord, since you have given me strength.' Because Daniel knows of the Lord's triumph in the battle with principalities and powers, he is prepared for the lesser national conflicts that lie ahead, which is what chapter 11 is all about.

2. The Kings of the South and the North (chapter 11)

Daniel 11 is one of the longest chapters in the book, and certainly the most difficult for any preacher. It is mainly about kings, and two of the principal kings come from the South and from the North. The obvious question arises: South of what, and north of what? The answer, of course, is, Of the people of God. The Lord's covenant community under the Old Testament lived in one geographical area, the land of Israel with Jerusalem as its capital. It is that people who are the target of the king of Egypt in the south and of Syria in the north. At the end of the chapter the people of God are again the target of the king of the latter days (vv.36ff.): 'He will also invade the Beautiful Land' (v.41).

This chapter's perspective is that the centre of the universe as far as God is concerned is his people. The Bible's first sentence is, 'In the beginning God created the heavens and the earth.' The structure of that sentence is climactically emphatic—'and especially the earth'. Of the whole universe, God loves planet earth. As the Lord surveys the world, he homes in upon his people. When he considers a town, he is touched by the feelings of the infirmities of his people as they are scattered through that community. He sees this Christian woman whose husband has Alzheimer's disease. Two years ago he could repair television sets, and now he cannot even switch one on. She is doing everything for her husband, and all of omnipotent love is focused on that home and what that woman is doing for the one to whom she made promises as a young bride that he would be her husband 'till death us do part'. Also in that town there is a teenage boy who has started work in a garage. He is the butt of the men's horseplay, especially since they have discovered that he is religious. He stammers out something for his Saviour, and not a word falls to the ground. God is concerned for him too. Then there is a family of which the wife alone is a Christian, but because of God's endless love for her, in some special way her husband is sanctified. Her children too, though they are not Christians, are in that same way 'holy': that is, they have come into the orbit of the Saviour's loving interest (1 Corinthians 7:14). She continually pleads a promise, 'Believe on the Lord Jesus Christ, and thou shalt be saved, and thy house' (Acts 16:31 AV).

God focuses his love upon his people, and it really matters to him how the world deals with them. Let not a hair on their heads be touched! The Lord Jesus spoke some of his most sober words, repeated in three of the Gospels, when he said: 'But whoso shall offend one of these little ones that believe in me'—he is not referring here to children but to his own people—'it were better for him that a millstone were hanged about his neck, and that he were drowned in the depth of the sea' (Matthew 18:6 AV). Christians carry about the baggage of failure because of the ordinariness of their congregational lives, the way they are ignored by society, their negligible impact upon their communities, and the frailty and inconsistency of their testimony. Transcending those concerns, we are conscious of what little creatures we are, living on a tiny planet on the edge of a universe of unimaginable vastness. We have to remind ourselves continually of Genesis 1:1—'and especially the earth' which God created for his purpose—and say to ourselves, 'I matter to God. He really cares for me. I'm the apple of his eye. I in Christ am the centre of his universe; not the great kings to the north and south, but me. I am poor and needy, but the Lord thinks on me.'

We do not receive that encouragement from anything in the world. Christians are nonentities in the eyes of men and women. 'The reason the world does not know us is that it did not know him' (1 John 3:2). Wherever we look, to the four points of the compass, we see kings rising, extending their boundaries, battling with other kings, and declining. That is the picture of the future that Daniel is shown in chapter 11. No kings from north or south will usher in a world government or achieve Utopian peace. That is what the Lord Jesus Christ declares when he speaks of the future in Mark 13 and also in Matthew 24: 'You will hear of wars and rumours of wars, but see to it that you are not alarmed. Such things must happen, but the end is still to come. Nation will rise against nation, and kingdom against kingdom. There will be famines and earthquakes in various places. All these are the beginning of birth-pains' (Matthew 24:6-8). This has been world history, and it will characterise the story of fallen mankind until the end will come.

So the promise of the return from exile under Cyrus has been fulfilled. There are believers actually back in Jerusalem. Thousands will follow them. The seventy years' exile has come to an end. Is this going to be the beginning of a wonderful dawn for mankind—a new world order? That is how some may have been talking. Triumphalism is in the air, and so it has entered their theology. Then 'a revelation was given to Daniel . . . and it concerned a great war' (10:1). While the holy people are in the world, the world will hate the church as it hates the church's Lord. Whether you look to the north or south, the present or the future, the story is going to be of nations rising and falling, blood, sweat and tears. In this eleventh chapter Persia is mentioned by name (v.2), also Greece (v.2) and Egypt (v.7). All were extraordinary civilisations, but what they did was the very reverse of establishing world peace. 'The creation waits in eager expectation for the sons of God to be revealed' (Romans 8:19). Only then will 'the creation itself be liberated from its bondage to decay and brought into the glorious freedom of the children of God. We know that the whole creation has been groaning as in the pains of childbirth right up to the present time. Not only so, but we ourselves, who have the first-fruits of the Spirit, groan inwardly as we wait eagerly for our adoption as sons, the redemption of our bodies' (Romans 8:21-23). There can be no regeneration of all things by the kings of the earth. Alliances, dynastic marriages, the sacrifice of thousands of soldiers in the cause of world domination—all are of no avail in renewing creation.

There is an exactness about the prophecy of this chapter: it is only the actual names of the kings and some of their empires that are omitted. The three kings who appeared in Persia after Cyrus (v.2) were Cambyses, Smerdis and Darius Hystaspia. The 'fourth, who will be far richer than all the others' (v.2) was Xerxes. The attempted invasion of Greece was the height of Persian power. The 'mighty king' who appeared was Alexander the Great, whose empire was soon broken up into four divisions (v.4). The next stage is the rise of Egypt, 'the king of the South' (vv.5-20). The dynasty which ruled in Egypt after the breaking up of Alexander's kingdom was known as Ptolemaic, and that which ruled in Syria was known as Seleucid. Ptolemy Soter (322-305 BC) was the king of the South, and the prince mentioned is Seleucus. 'The daughter of the king of the South' was Berenice, who married Antiochus II, yet was unable to maintain herself against a rival wife, Laodice. Antiochus finally divorced her and Laodice encouraged her sons to murder Berenice. The 'one from her family line' (v.7) who arises and takes her place was her brother, who came against an army from the north and also succeeded in killing Laodice. The passage then goes on to relate the various struggles and wars between the Ptolemies and Seleucids until the appearance of Antiochus Epiphanes.

In the next section the book of Daniel returns to the rise and reign of Antiochus Epiphanes (vv.21-35). He is the 'contemptible person' who seizes the kingdom 'through intrigue' (v.21). He won over the support of the kings of Pergamus, and the Syrians gave in to him. His ability to 'act deceitfully' (v.23) earned him the nickname of 'Epimanes' ('madman') instead of the title which he himself assumed—'Epiphanes' ('illustrious'). His Egyptian campaigns are mentioned (vv.25-29), and after the first of three were completed he set his heart 'against the holy covenant' (v.28), i.e. the land of Palestine. All of this is seen as coming 'at the appointed time' (vv.27,29). God is in control of every detail.

Antiochus failed in his third invasion of Egypt because of Rome's nautical intervention: 'Ships of the western coastlands will oppose him, and he will lose heart' (v.30). So he turned in his fury on Palestine. Jerusalem was invaded on the Sabbath, a heathen altar was erected on the altar of burnt offering, and the daily sacrifices ended. There were apostate Jews in league with Antiochus and they carried out his designs; 'but the people who know their god will firmly resist him' (v.32). Teachers arose and instructed the people, though they were fearfully persecuted. But 'when they fall,

136

they will receive a little help' (v.34). This apparently refers to Judas Maccabaeus, whose rebellion proved to be successful, so that on 25 December 165 BC the altar of the temple was rededicated.

The final section in this chapter of warfare (vv.36-45) takes the persecution of the church by Antiochus to a higher plane. He becomes a prefigurement of future persecution by a more notorious person, the one referred to in the New Testament as 'the man of lawlessness' (2 Thessalonians 2:3). Antiochus persecuted the church shortly before the first advent of Christ, while the antichrist will persecute the church before his second advent. In verses 21-35 Antiochus is not once spoken of individually as a 'king', except when his negotiations with another are mentioned and 'the two kings' are referred to collectively (v.27). He is called 'a contemptible person' (v.21), and then merely denoted as 'he'. Anything that would serve to dignify him is avoided. But the figure in verses 36-39 is specifically called 'the king'. His threat to the church will be marked by four characteristics:

1. 'He will show no regard to the gods of his fathers . . . nor will he regard any god' (v.37). Agnosticism or atheism will be the common cultural attitude.

2. The 'desire of women' will not be held in regard (v.37 AV). That desire is for human and family love and is an example of the best of true humanity. A disdain of tenderness will characterise personal relations at that period. In the Russian Revolution various leaders adopted strong names to show their superiority to mere men: for example, 'Stalin' ('steel') and 'Molotov' ('hammer').

137

3. 'He . . . will exalt himself above . . . all [the gods]' (v.37). There will be self-assertion to the point of self-deification.

4. He 'will honour a god of fortresses'. He is the personification of human strength. War will be his god, and he will support warfare with all that he has (v.38). 'There is always some Carthage that must be destroyed for some Rome to be free for its own brand of slavery' (R. J. Rushdoony, *Thy Kingdom Come: Studies in Daniel and Revelation*, p.77).

The final five verses illustrate the symbolism of this section (vv.40-45). The nations of Edom, Moab and Ammon are long-dead states and peoples. They are not going to be reconstituted ever again. At the end of the present age the antichrist will engage in fierce conflict for the control of world powers. They are symbolised in the powers which Daniel and his readers know— Edom, Moab and Ammon. 'He will pitch his royal tents between the seas and the beautiful holy mountain' (v.45). The sea symbolises the world (Daniel 7:2; Revelation 17:15), and the 'beautiful holy mountain' is a frequent type of the true church. The antichrist will seek to straddle the two, church and world, with an open door to both, and so syncretistically control them, breaking down the barrier between them. 'Yet he will come to his end, and no-one will help him' (v.45).

All this history is summarised so fully because, at the rise of Antiochus Epiphanes and of the antichrist, the covenant people of God will need this knowledge as a balm and rationale for action. Such knowledge will keep them sane and faithful through everything they are going to face. The unusual fact about this chapter is that in the first 27 verses not a word is recorded about the church; but the events that occurred were affecting the very existence of the people of God and the coming Redeemer, and so the Lord is involved. That is why such attention is paid to the rise and fall of these nations. The Scriptures do not describe what was happening in the great Inca civilisation of Peru. They do not tell us what was going on in China or in India. This silence does not infer that these civilisations were unimportant or lacking in colossal achievements, but that in those years their cultures had no effect upon the redeemed people of God. The Bible is a history of redemption, of the Saviour and of the saved, and it was whenever the world brushed God's people that the events were recorded. Everything revolved around the holy people and the Holy Land. The church and its Lord are the mid-point of human history.

Someone has said that 'history is the scaffolding' God uses to build his temple. As soon as the last of the people of God are added to this temple, there will be no further need of scaffolding, nor of the labourers who helped with the building. There will be no need any longer for the kings of the North and the South, the kings of Persia, Greece and Egypt, no need for Alexander, Philip of Macedonia and Antiochus Epiphanes. When Christ comes again, there will be no need for preachers and missionaries, once that last stone has been placed upon the temple to shouts of grace.

All that happens at every point of the compass, if it touches God's people, must work for their good. When the Romans and the Jews worked together to crucify our Lord Jesus Christ, it was according to God's determinate counsel and foreknowledge. It was also working for our good. Everything happens for the sake of the church. We are the meaning of Golgotha. It is because of God's goal for the church that events happen to us as they do. All things revolve around the church.

The first half of this chapter records a sad time in world history, when the church was being ignored. The voice of the prophet was silent, and there was little expectation. The church was compromising with the world, and was ignored by it. The salt was losing its savour. God's people were silent about the Lord, and so the Word of God is silent about them. When Antiochus Epiphanes re-emerges in the narrative he becomes a sort of icon, a figure that comes to personify and en-flesh the powers of evil. He points forward to the coming 'man of sin'. It is fascinating to contrast him with the Lord Jesus Christ. In the Old Testament the Saviour is foreshadowed by many figures, such as Melchizedec, Moses, David and Solomon, and we see Christ in them, albeit through a glass darkly. We are conscious of all the graces that the Spirit of Christ in them had conceived, and in them we find the Lord Jesus. But there is only one prefigurement of the antichrist in the Old Testament, and that is Antiochus Epiphanes IV.

This book of Daniel returns to the figure of Antiochus Epiphanes on a number of occasions. What is this teaching us? What do we do when such a figure is about? How do we act when evil marches through the land? Two things:

- Resist! 'The people who know their God will firmly resist him' (v.32). The subversive church is always a resistance movement.
- Teach! 'Those who are wise will instruct many'

(v.33). We insist upon an educated faith. We give people knowledge and discernment. We build them up in any and every legitimate way. Literature, preaching, discussion groups, camps, conferences—everything we can do to commend the Word of God—'teaching them to obey everything I have commanded you' (Matthew 28:20). The survival kit of the resistance movement is the Bible. It is alive and powerful. It is spirit and life.

There is great fascination now with a newly elected government, so-called New Labour. There is some perplexity as to what New Labour actually believes. What are its policies and the ideological principles of government? The honeymoon period—the first hundred days—has come to an end; and what of the tough times that every government faces? Austin Mitchell, the Labour Member of Parliament for Grimsby, explained his concerns for his party with this question: Does it have sufficient ideology to take it through the hard times? That is the test of any movement, isn't it? Certainly it is the test of the gospel church of the Lord Jesus Christ. This chapter is full of prophecies of tough times ahead. How do we survive? Resist and teach! You survive great tribulations by the Word of God.

3. Resurrection hope (chapter 12)

The story of Daniel cannot end with the destruction of antichrist, because the mighty works of God do not end there. The climax is doxology. The Book of Revelation ends with a choir singing praise to God. It is not enough that the enemy of God is conquered. What is creaturely power before omnipotence? What other

141

outcome could there be? You do not magnify God by saying he succeeded in crushing a worm. The book of Daniel ends with the cosmic triumph of Christ over death itself, and the last chapter contains a message of new covenant hope. 'But at that time your people— everyone whose name is found written in the book— will be delivered. Multitudes who sleep in the dust of the earth will awake' (vv.1-2). This will occur 'at that time'—that is, when antichrist is destroyed, then resurrection glory begins. The deliverance comes not by the heroic courage of men but by an act of God. The Lord of hosts, and with him all his holy angels led by Michael the great prince, 'will arise' (v.1). That is how the twelfth chapter commences.

The hosts of heaven have waited long for 'that time'—the angels poised on the ramparts of heaven, their weapons ready, waiting on their Lord's sign, that they may come in their legions and deliver God's people and assist in the raising of the dead. They are grieved at all they have witnessed. The innumerable company of heaven has longed for the trumpet blast to sound the attack. 'The angel of the LORD encamps around those who fear him, and he delivers them' (Psalm 34:7). In our day Christendom is worshipping angels; angelolatry is one of the heresies of the age. We do not react against that by ignoring what the Bible says about these servants of God who are ministering spirits to the church. We experience something of the fulfilment of the promise, 'For he will command his angels concerning you to guard you in all your ways; they will lift you up in their hands, so that you will not strike your foot against a stone' (Psalm 91:11-12). I remember putting a tiny grandson on a sledge on a slippery slope and letting him go off. To my horror he went like lightning

142

towards an opening where there were cars going back and forth, myself running in slow motion behind him, crying from my heart that God would spare him. The sledge veered off the path into a post, leaving him with a black eye and myself with a broken spirit. God sent his angel to protect him. How many dangers have we been delivered from? There was one who refused the help of angels when he hung on the tree, in order that we might have their unseen support and ministry day by day. He struggled with demons so that we could be surrounded by angels.

Who are those that are going to be delivered? 'Everyone whose name is found written in the book' (v.1). This Lamb's Book of Life records all that the Father gave to the Son in a donation of grace and love before the foundation of the world. They also have their names written on the palms of Christ's hands in marks of indelible grace. The same names were on his heart when he refused to end the enfleshment and come down from the cruel cross. Some people have a singular obsession that their names are recorded in somebody's will. The Christian has learned that he cannot serve God and mammon, and his hope is that he is a true believer because his name is written in the book. The Christian cannot read that volume while he is in the world, but there is another book that the Christian may read, and that is the Bible. Wherever the Christian sees 'sinner' and 'ungodly', there he reads his own name. Every time he sees a description of a believer, what a believer believes, and how a believer lives, he prays, 'O enable me to believe this! Enable me to live like this!' That is the principal means of attaining the assurance that our names are recorded in the Lamb's Book of Life.

143

There was once a Christian Welshman called Cadwaladr Jenkins, and Cadwaladr Jenkins had no assurance of salvation. This went on for months and even years, and that he was not saved was his constant fear. Then one night he had the most wonderful dream. He was caught up into heaven and he entered a great hall of glory, where he saw a table on which lay a huge book. He walked up to the book and opened it, turning the pages to the letter 'J'. He went down with his finger past the Jameses to the Jenkinses and there, finally, in letters of gold he read the name 'Cadwaladr Jenkins'. His own name recorded there! He woke up the next morning overwhelmed with joy and walked on air all morning. At noon the doorbell went. At the door stood a stranger, and when he spoke he had an Australian accent. Cadwaladr asked, 'Yes, what can I do for you?' The stranger said, 'Do you remember that many decades ago your father's younger brother emigrated to Australia?' 'Yes, I do remember him telling me that', said Cadwaladr. 'Well, I am his son, and your cousin.' 'My cousin?' said a dumbstruck Cadwaladr. 'I've come back for the first time to meet my family here.' 'Come in; come in!' said Cadwaladr. 'What's your name?' 'Well,' his cousin said shyly, 'my father loved your name so much that he called me Cadwaladr Jenkins too.' With that knowledge, all the joy and assurance that the dream had given the Welshman evaporated in a moment!

No mortal can ever read the Lamb's Book of Life before he enters the dwelling place of the King, but as he reads this Bible day by day every true Christian will say, 'Now that is what I believe by grace, and that is how I want to live.' God will help us, and on the basis of this testimony of the Word of God a growing confidence will be ours. The Spirit by the Word will bear witness with our own spirits that we are children of God.

What will happen when the angels come at the trumpet of God? 'Multitudes who sleep in the dust of the earth will awake: some to everlasting life' (v.2). Their sleep is over, and in the twinkling of an eye they will be changed at the last trump. This corruptible must put on incorruption; this mortal must put on immortality. The logic of the resurrection of the Lord Christ demands it: 'awake . . . to everlasting life!' But there is another resurrection—'others to shame and everlasting contempt' (v.2). Many of those men and women had indulged their bodies, giving in to every desire. They filled themselves with alcohol. They gorged themselves with food. They injected themselves with drugs, which they snorted, smoked, chewed, inhaled and swallowed. They pampered and besotted their bodies. Their god was their belly, and in the end they hated their bodies with all their lusts, passions and cravings. They sighed in their dark night and thought it would be good to be dead. 'Welcome, sweet sleep! We shall be glad to finish with these insatiable bodies for ever.' But when God comes on that tremendous day and all his holy angels with him, their bodies will rise again—the addict's body and the drunkard's body. Casanova's body will rise again. And what hateful bodies they will be in that day, rising to shame and everlasting contempt! Monstrous and misshapen bodies, manifest with all the ugliness of sin unchecked by God's common grace—revolting bodies! All that is of the divine image, all the restraints of God's goodness to all people, removed for ever! Christ said it will be so. He who cannot lie declared it. 'Marvel not at this: for the hour is coming, in the which all that are in the graves shall hear his voice, and shall come forth; they that have done good, unto the resurrection of life; and they that have done evil, unto the resurrection of damnation' (John 5:28-29 AV). The God who cannot lie said those words.

Those in the Lamb's Book of Life will enjoy everlasting life. 'Those who are wise will shine like the brightness of the heavens' (v.3). A footnote in the NIV suggests the alternative translation, 'those who impart wisdom'. Not only are they wise, but they commend wisdom to others. What is wisdom? To fear the Lord is its beginning, and in the treasures of the Bible it is sustained. Its embodiment is found in the Word who became flesh. That wisdom is theirs, and that is what they impart, impressing it upon their children and upon all over whom they have any influence. Their concern is for people to be wise. We have all met men who obviously spend a great deal on their personal appearance. Their hair is cut in a certain way, their jewellery, the lotions they put on themselves, the expensive clothes they wear, their shoes, and even the body-piercing—all is carefully chosen for self-promotion. But their appearance is to no avail, because when you meet them they are characterised by folly. They are ignorant about the ABC of life. Who am I? What is man's chief end? What is the good life? Who is God? How can I be saved? What is death? What lies beyond? The unwise cannot answer those questions; they have nothing to give. It is 'those who impart wisdom who will shine like the brightness of the heavens' (v.3). These are the people who can 'lead many to righteousness' (v.3). So those whose names are in the Lamb's Book of Life are passionately concerned about other people. The definition of the goal of evangelism here is leading dying sinners to righteousness. Those who will be raised to everlasting life will shine like the stars for ever and ever.

The church always has such luminaries. No Christian has any lack of them. I have always had 'stars' in my firmament. Over forty years ago, when grace first changed my life, I began to discover them: an Inter Schools Christian Fellowship worker, some fellow pupils, a much teased teacher, camp officers, students at Cardiff University, professors at Westminster Seminary, and even some preachers! Today a number lead the church where I am pastor. They will never know they were my heroes and everything I'd like to be. So I fly higher than an eagle; they are the wind beneath my wings. Every Christian can think of a cluster of stars beaming away constantly serving God in Kenya or Sicily or Cyprus. It is a tough vocation, but they shine like stars in the universe as they hold out the word of life (Philippians 2:15-16). How dark our world would be without them! How tough it would be to steer a straight course without such reference points!

This long revelation from the Holy One is finally coming to an end. 'Close up and seal the words of the scroll', he says to Daniel (v.4). So this panorama of history that began at the end of chapter 10 finishes. When Daniel has heard it all he is conscious that two others—perhaps two divine witnesses confirming the truth of what has been said—have also been listening intently. One of them now speaks up and the question he asks is, 'How long will it be before these astonishing things are fulfilled?' (v.6). It is the question that Daniel's predecessor Isaiah asked when he received his tough commission: 'For how long, O Lord?' (Isaiah 6:11). It is the question asked by many of the psalmists: 'How long will it be?' (Psalm 90:13). My vocation from God may

147

be to serve him in a barren place facing a future full of trials, but I know that this is exactly where God has put me, so I am not going to complain. I have learned, in whatsoever state I am, to be content. I am allowed to ask, How long?

The strange answer is, 'It will be for a time, times and half a time' (v.7). We wonder if Daniel was satisfied. Who would be content with that answer? Daniel is told more, something he did not ask: 'When the power of the holy people has been finally broken, all these things will be completed' (v.7). Holy people have power. They are energised by an indwelling Saviour. They have unlimited access to Omnipotence. They can do all things through Christ who strengthens them. They can feed their enemies when they hunger; they can forgive seventy times seven; they can go the second mile; they can keep their marriage vows; they can love one another with pure hearts fervently. Those among them who are strong can bear the burdens of the weak. Each one of them deems the other better than himself. Christians are so strong that they will inherit the earth. The devil and his minions seek to destroy such strengths. Perilous times come when they are under attack. Jesus asks, 'when the Son of Man comes, will he find faith [faith that is powerful] on the earth?' (Luke 18:8).

'How long will it be?' The answer was for a time, times and half a time. Daniel did not understand the reply. It has not been given to the church to know the time of the end because it is not important for us to know it. The logic is that in an hour when you do not expect him the Son of Man will come, so be always ready (Matthew 24:24). Daniel is told this: 'a time'—a time when another antichrist establishes his kingdom;

and 'times'—double the affliction, twice the intensity of grief and the fiery furnace, when the church desperately looks for deliverance; and 'half a time'—even worse, when the power of God's people is finally broken and the love of many grows cold—and *then* deliverance comes. 'Half a time' was the period when one antichrist said he had set up a Reich that would last a thousand years: it lasted twelve years. He comes—the Lord Jesus is coming. When the church is at its weakest and congregations think, 'He will not come for us because we are so weak. How we let him down! How unprofitable we are! He wouldn't come for me'—it is exactly then that he comes for us.

Daniel tells us, 'I heard, but I did not understand' (v.8). He had walked with God all his life; he had the charisma of prophecy and could interpret great mysteries with the fullest accuracy and authority; but he was also a man of like passions as ourselves. There were truths that came to him from God, and however much he exercised his mind about them, he ultimately shook his head in ignorance before them. Isn't that encouraging to everyone? We have this Book with its great profundities, and we sometimes feel like Sir Isaac Newton —as if we were standing before a vast ocean picking up one or two pebbles.

God says to him, 'Go your way, Daniel, because the words are closed up and sealed until the time of the end' (v.9). The Word of God is settled and complete. Heaven and earth may go out of fashion, but this Book will never become passé. All that it records is going to be accomplished, but as for the actual time of that accomplishment, no man needs to know. 'None of the wicked will understand, but those who are wise will understand' (v.10). 'Go your way, Daniel', God says (v.9)—and then repeats the exhortation, 'As for you, go your way till the end' (v.13). He is exhorting Daniel not to worry about the times and the seasons, but to go on his way through life as a servant of God. It is the greatest blessing to have found this way. Many never find it, living lives without purpose and without shape. They are guided by their own feelings into spontaneous actions that are frequently destructive. They have relationships at whim, religion at whim, employment at whim, and all their behaviour at a whim. They expect preternatural nudges and hunches to accompany them always, and they will be persuaded that they are from the living God. But Daniel had a way on which he had travelled from youth, and now as an old man God is saying to him, 'Carry on.' He found the way and never left it. It was leading him to life. The Lord Jesus Christ said, 'I am the way.' That way is explained in the Word of God. There can be no greater fulfilment in life than to find that way and then to go on it until the end. 'Go your way!'

How long did Antiochus Epiphanes dominate Jerusalem? Between 1,290 and 1,335 days (vv.11-12), that is, about three and a half years. Not decades or centuries—just a matter of days, and that frightening evil was overthrown. Satan's little season is quickly gone. 'Blessed is the one who waits for and reaches the end of the . . . days' (v.12). Let us keep going on our way, though it sometimes leads through Vanity Fair, into the Valley of the Shadow, across Enchanted Ground and up Hill Difficulty, because that is the way God has prescribed. It is a good way and a holy way, and the weariness we experience on it is much to be preferred to the sloth of the sluggard. 'You will rest,' Daniel is assured, 'and then at the end of the days you will rise to receive

150

your allotted inheritance' (v.13). That is where the way ends, with an inheritance incorruptible, undefiled and that fades not away, reserved in heaven for us (1 Peter 1:4). That allotted span is quickly over, and 'it were a well-spent journey, though seven deaths lay between'. It will be all over in the twinkling of an eye; we shall soon be meeting at Jesus' feet. Let all who read these words make sure that they are found in Christ and ready in that great day!